It's All About Kids!

Every Child Deserves a "Teacher of the Year"

Debbie Happy Cohen
& the Faculty and Staff of
Independent Day School: Corbett Campus

Bee Happy Publishing
Tampa, Florida

First edition published in 2003
by Bee Happy Publishing, Tampa, FL
an imprint of Total Success Coaching, Inc.
2300 N.E. 196 Street, Miami, FL 33180
Telephone (813) 931-7707

Manufactured in the United States of America
Copyright ©2003 Independent Day School

Editor: Willy Mathes
Layout Design and Proof Editor: Tery Robertson
Cover Designer: Steven Lisi
Photographer: Joseph Spagnuolo

Table of Contents

Foreword: A+ Action Approach iii

Prologue: 500 Years Later 1

PART I: AN EXTRA-ORDINARY BEGINNING 7

Flat-Earth Thinkers 8

The Explorers of 1968: "Two Silly Ladies" 12

Putting Kids First 21

Finding the Right Leaders 25

The Root of a Happy Child 36

A Supportive Board Lives the Philosophy 38

The Makings of a Leader 41

Four Golden Rules to Hire and Keep the Best Staff 44

Training Makes a Difference: The *M.O.R.E.*
   Approach 49

Surviving Stormy Seas: Learning to Deal
   with Resistance 55

The Tide Turns with a Charted Course 66

PART II: LIVING THE PHILOSOPHY 71

A Three-Pronged Approach 72

The *M.O.R.E. Approach* is All About Staff
   Development 75

More on the *M.O.R.E. Approach* 78

Lesson Planning and Life's Lessons Have a Lot
   in Common 80

Innovation Requires Change 84

PART III: EDU-TALK: TEACHER STORIES 89

Balancing Novelty and Routine in Lesson
  Planning 91
Group Dynamics -- Making Connections: *Personal and
  Professional Growth for Kids* 123
Behavioral Lessons: *Social, Emotional and
  Academic* 139
Empowerment for Teachers, Parents and the
  Community: *Personal and Professional
  Joy and Satisfaction* 158

PART IV: "IDS PRESS" STORIES 175

The Evolution of the IDS Warrior 177
Primary Programs 180
Intermediate Programs 190
Middle School Programs 199
School-wide Programs 209
Community Service & Training for Excellence 217

A Summary of the 7 Components of the
  M.O.R.E. Approach 223
Resources 225
Media Resources 229
IDS Philosophy 230
Catch the Spirit at IDS! 231
Services Available 232

Foreword

This book was written because it just seemed like the right thing to do. We believed that there was information to be shared with parents, educators, and anyone interested in the realm of education. It was also written because we are excited about what we're doing at IDS, and want to share some of our lessons learned. It is our hope that this book will inspire or reinforce the work of others, or enlist volunteers in the quest to accelerate the learning process so that it is more joyful and challenging, more stimulating and productive, more nurturing with high standards and high expectations.

The book has evolved into a story of leadership lessons past and present, the excitement, and trials and tribulations through the change process, and the energy and feelings that come from a journey that continually focuses on children first.

It is often believed that to have success, it is necessary to first set a goal, and then go for it by following a set of procedures or several recommended steps to achieve the desired outcome. Actually, that may work for some, but that neat pattern may be more theoretical than real. Common components may arise, but order, set patterns and expectations of what is to come are often interrupted by the unexpected. And that, indeed, is what has occurred over the years at Independent Day School, where patterns of leadership and change have emerged, some by accident and some on purpose. Yet, common characteristics in the process have always been present, whether they were led by parents, administrators, teachers, the Board of Trustees, or any combination of the four. The common thread that always steered the ship, over time, remained the belief in "children first" – thus the name for this book, "It's All About Kids."

The thirty-five year old voyage of this school had maps to chart the direction that were always as good as the most up to date knowledge available at the time. In recent years, research in education has become available to support and/or to reject intuitive beliefs about how best to learn.

The book offers five sections for consideration on leadership, change, and innovation.

The Prologue describes a quantum leap from the past to the present, linking a flat-earth versus round-earth mentality to limitations and possibilities affecting schools and education today.

Part I uses a story format to tell the rich and diverse history of the evolution of a little school, always trying to make a huge difference in the big world.

Part II describes how we translate the philosophy into action through a reliance on leading-edge brain research and best practices in education, along with a lesson-planning approach that has an immediate and direct connection to life's lessons. The development and explanation of the *M.O.R.E. Approach (Multiple Options for Results in Education)* for training and learning is also described in this section.

Part III highlights teachers, their stories, and an "abundance mentality" of ideas that arise from planning lessons, which are consistently vibrant and exciting, while at the same time balanced with comfort, connections and tradition.

Part IV captures a snapshot of the school through a variety of Press Releases that shed light around the myriad of opportunities that create an enviable context for learning.

In addition to the four parts, the diagram on the next page describes the A+ Action Approach to Leadership and Change. Through months of examining the history of IDS, it became apparent that seven common characteristics consistently appeared in the school's transformation and evolution. Each component went beyond words and ideas, translating into action steps that propelled the school forward.

At the end of the Prologue and each section of Part I, Leadership Lessons summarize the section and incorporate the components of the A+ Action Approach to Leadership and Change.

Today, IDS functions with an unwavering resolve to do whatever it takes "to improve the schools of today and invent the schools of tomorrow." as suggested by Dr. William Katzenmeyer, former Dean of Education at the University of South Florida. The following pages do just what we aim to do every day for our students; and that is, to give the reader multiple ways to learn about our school and grasp the intent of our journey: to discover the *Cape of Exceptional Learning.*

Dr. Joyce Burick Swarzman
Headmaster

P.S. A big "thank you" goes to Pam Sims, whose award-winning book, <u>Awakening Brilliance</u>, inspired the format for Part I. A big thank you to Oprah Winfrey, whose life and work has encouraged millions to start to read again and to even think about writing. A big "thank you" to the <u>Chicken Soup for the Soul</u> team, who trained Debbie Cohen in a way that inspired her to want to search out positive models that would be an inspiration to others to perhaps follow. A big "thank you" to Ken Blanchard and his team, whose parable-approach to writing inspires a healthy, joyful approach to leadership, through which we can all learn. An inspiring idea began this school in 1968. Inspiring ideas continue to call us into action.

An A+ Action Approach
to Leadership and Change

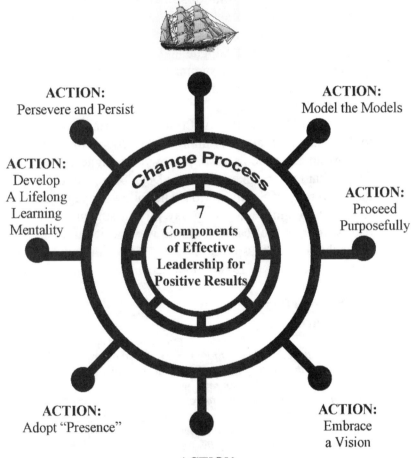

ACTION:
Persevere and Persist

ACTION:
Model the Models

ACTION:
Develop
A Lifelong
Learning
Mentality

ACTION:
Proceed
Purposefully

Change Process

7
Components
of Effective
Leadership for
Positive Results

ACTION:
Adopt "Presence"

ACTION:
Embrace
a Vision

ACTION:
Build Leadership Capacity,
Teams and Networks

PROLOGUE
"500 Years Later"

*A Back to School Night Presentation
at Independent Day School (IDS)
Given by Dr. Joyce Burick Swarzman, Headmaster
September 1999*

This is a very special year. This year marks many lasts and many firsts. For example, this is obviously the last time we will welcome you to a school year that begins with 1900-and-something, and this is the first time we will welcome you to a school year that will begin with a 2000. I have found the study of what happens during "turns of centuries" to be fascinating. The decades prior to and following the transition from century to century are marked by rapid change, some major impacts on the progress of the world, and unexpected surprises.

Something else amazed me this summer that prompted this speech.

My husband and I flew to Portugal in June, before embarking on a cruise. After flying for hours, our first morning began with a bus tour of Lisbon. Fighting a serious case of jet lag, I listened half-heartedly to the tour guide discuss the impact on the world made by Portuguese explorers living 500 years ago. "Explorers? Oh, help!" The last time I thought about Portuguese explorers was during fifth grade tests while drawing Old World Maps in Mrs. Reynolds' class at Jefferson Elementary School in Dayton, Ohio!

Our tour group disembarked the bus at the Portuguese Maritime Museum for an hour-long tour of historic explorers through modern times. "Ugh," I thought, but something incredible happened in the next hour that changed my entire perspective.

We walked into a large room facing a huge map of the world, which hung from a long, tall wall. I heard the guide in the background talk about the explorer Vasco da Gama and how his quest for the riches and spices of the Indies led to his discovery of the route around the Cape of Good Hope.

Suddenly, I felt a "rush of clarity." Five hundred years ago, during the transition from the 15th to the 16th Century, explorers were altering lifestyles, the economy, human relations, and expanding possibilities. Beginning to sense a similarity between then and now, my curiosity was piqued.

As the tour group wandered from the room, I stayed and studied the map. I reached up and traced the routes that these explorers had sailed. I had some major insights that seemed to make interesting connections to our world today, especially to the world of education.

1)   Although these explorers loved adventure, they had a goal: to discover a faster, better and less expensive way to transport goods that would enhance daily life and basic survival. Back then, spices were in high demand, especially the ones from the Indies. So some explorers were motivated to find a quicker, less costly route to get the riches.

2)   Only some shared the vision. Before Vasco da Gama's 1497 journey began, other explorers had attempted to prove that the earth was round and that one could actually sail around it. But still there were "Flat-Earth People" who fought the future, vowed that it would never work and declared that exploration would cost too much.

They did much to dissuade the kings and queens from sponsoring these voyages. Some "Flat-Earthers" even used religion to bolster their points of view and fears of tomorrow.

3) There were those who persisted, dreamed and kept going, based upon the results of those explorers who had gone before them, discovering great lands, new vistas, wealth and opportunity. Still, the great route to the Indies remained yet to be discovered.

4) These trips cost big bucks; therefore, the lead explorers had to persuade those with the money, the kings and queens of the time, to support their journeys. Thank goodness for us today that, over 500 years ago, there were leaders who *financed the visions* and *supported the trailblazers*. During this period, the Portuguese monarchy included visionaries who were financially supportive of these expeditions and who, in turn, received wealth even beyond their expectations.

5) Almost one year after setting sail, on May 18, 1498, Vasco da Gama and his fleet first sighted the Malabar Coast of India; three days later, they arrived in Calicut.

With this one trip around the Cape of Good Hope, the entire economic system of the world subsequently changed! Five hundred years ago, at the turn of the century, Vasco's route to India permitted lower prices, faster delivery to merchants and greater riches, as a new and better-equipped shipping industry took over!

Long, expansive land routes used to transport goods were eventually wiped out. Both large and small businesses along these land routes that had been the expensive distribution centers for spices and other goods were most likely downsized or eliminated.

Now, I ask all of you in this room, how many of us are in work that was once thought to be forever needed, but now is in danger of either 1) cutbacks or 2) extinction? In fact, I bet that, back then, it was like the current typewriter businesses over the last 8 to 10 years – gone, kaput, no longer needed, wiped out or slowly being "phased out," with one or two typewriters hanging around for small jobs. Just try to get a ribbon or find 'typewriter' in the phone book!

Poof! One major trip around Africa and life as the world knew it changed. But remember, lots of work and travels led up to that historic journey. Lots of discoveries came before and many came after.

After staring at this map, taking a mental journey back in time, I meandered through the museum, studying models of ships, noting their sails, carefully identifying how improving the sails allowed subsequent journeys to be faster, easier, safer and more productive, and maybe even more fun!

So what does all of this mean for us today, for you as parents, for us as teachers? What does this mean for our children and the future?

I predict your children and your grandchildren will be living with the riches being discovered today. Very soon, the explosion of information about the brain and how it works will be commonplace.

At IDS, we are searching for the educational route to success for all children. Our goal is to find the "Cape of Exceptional Learning" and travel there with all of the best intentions, using a compass that is directed toward success and achievement, both academically and personally.

I feel that we resemble the Portuguese explorers who were the best in their era. They studied with a core of navigators, learned from the trips of others and, as a team, worked to perfect their discoveries and innovations. We, at IDS, do the same.

Sitting before you is one of the best, most highly trained faculties in the world. I encourage you to support them as they sail their 'ships.' Question how your young 'explorer' is doing – question often, and send information to help us navigate a successful journey for your child.

I believe that, within the next one or two decades, the Pentium or e-mail of learning will be discovered. The rough routes of learning for some will be wiped out by newer, faster, more gentle and effortless strategies.

We at IDS live every day to help bring your child's education closer to that magical route, while at the same time traveling with the best equipment known to us today. We face a monumental task: integrating current, effective teaching methods with leading-edge techniques in learning. You can count on us to always work toward solutions.

Please allow our teachers to teach; have confidence in the decision that you made for your child to receive a world class education. Teachers will decide where the furniture goes and in which rooms students learn. Teachers will choose the best strategies to achieve the course of study, all designed to take place in a very caring, nurturing environment. Do speak to us about your child, and give us the barometer of how he or she is doing in order to help us navigate a successful journey for him or her. Then we will sail together toward what we all want: well-educated, happy children and happy teachers.

Our fleet is built upon the experiences, research and intuition of others, as well as our own discoveries and efforts to reach the Cape of Exceptional Learning. It is with great pride, appreciation and gratitude for all they do that I introduce you to the faculty and staff at IDS.

A+ Action Approach
Leadership Lessons

➤ **Embrace a Vision**
The explorers led by sustaining a compelling idea that held enough power and possibility that they were willing to proceed. Effective leaders seek to inspire the population to embrace a vision of greater possibilities. Wise leadership expects resistance and, therefore, is ready to utilize inspiration, conviction and often intuition to hold true to the vision, while steering change in a progressive direction.

➤ **Model the Models**
500 years ago, explorers produced a model for developing early "think tanks" for reaching goals that seemed outrageous and impossible at the time. Their successes inspired people to move from a 'Flat-Earth' mentality to 'Round Earth' thinking, pointing the way for the paradigm shifts of today.

PART I

An Extra-Ordinary Beginning
A History of Independent Day School
Corbett Campus
Recounted in a Novel Way

"Exploration is wired into our brains. If we can see the horizon, we want to know what's beyond."
-- *Buzz Aldrin,* **Astronaut**

"Having courage doesn't mean you're not afraid of doing something. It means you are afraid, but you do it anyway."
-- *Eleanor Roosevelt,* **First Lady**

"It's a funny thing about life; if you refuse to accept anything but the best, you very often get it."
-- *W. Somerset Maugham,* **Author**

Flat-Earth Thinkers

"Grandma Betty, what's a 'flat-earth thinker?'" seven-year old Johnny asked, as he jumped over a puddle, trying not to get his shiny new shoes dirty.

The stars shined brightly as Betty, Marilyn and their three grandchildren leisurely made their way to Marilyn's car. The two women glowed with pride, as they silently reflected about the 35-year anniversary celebration they had just attended, where they were honored for the school they had founded. It had been a beautiful day that would be remembered by many.

Since Betty was visiting from out of town, and it had been years since the two ladies had gotten a chance to see each other, they decided to go out for ice cream after the big event. Both women were looking forward to spending time together.

"Do you always have to ask so many questions, Johnny?" Johnny's sister Danielle, a brunette, 12-year-old know-it-all, asked impatiently. "I think I'm going to have bubble gum, chocolate and cookie-dough ice cream in a banana split," she thought out loud.

Marilyn, a bright-eyed, gracious, smartly dressed woman with light-brown hair, opened the door for Betty, a down-to-earth, silvery-gray haired, taller woman, who joined her in the front seat. Michael, Marilyn's handsome, blonde 21-year old grandson, and Betty's two grandchildren scooted into the roomy back seat of the light blue Chevrolet.

Pulling the car out of the parking lot, Betty looked at her freckle-faced grandson Johnny in the rear-view mirror. Staring briefly into his eager, young eyes, she began to address his earlier question. His inquiry had been sparked by a familiar message once again driven home by the school's current headmaster, Dr. Joyce Burick Swarzman, during her speech delivered that evening. Marilyn responded, "Well, you see, Johnny, flat-earth thinkers are people who believe only in what they can see." She then addressed her eldest grandson, "Mike, I'm sure you know people who get scared of the unknown and who resist new ideas, even though they might be good ones."

"Yeah," Mike replied, "like mom, who says she can live without e-mail!"

Marilyn laughed, "Exactly... except when she complains about being left out of the loop on some of our family news!"

"Could you imagine," Mike added, "if Christopher Columbus or the early explorers had e-mail?" He turned to Danielle and asked, "What do you remember learning in school about Christopher Columbus and his voyages?"

Danielle replied, "Well, I remember he was searching for the West Indies, but discovered America instead!" She looked to see whether or not she was on track with where Mike was going with the conversation. Seeing the encouraging look on his face, she went on. "People back home were afraid that he would fall off the earth because they believed the earth was flat."

Marilyn added, "That's right. But if they'd had e-mail, just imagine! He and many other explorers, like Vasco da Gama, could have e-mailed to let everyone know that they were okay!"

"It sounds like it was dangerous," Johnny said. "Why did they want to discover new lands so badly?"

"Well, Johnny..." Mike started to reply, but stopped short because, as they were pulling into the parking lot, they all noticed an unusually short line outside the ice cream parlor. It looked like people were leaving without any ice cream.

Danielle got out of the car to find out what was happening. She came back and reported, "The line is so short because the only flavors they have left are chocolate, vanilla and strawberry."

"What flavor do you want, Johnny?" Mike asked.

"I want chocolate-chip cookie dough. I don't want chocolate or vanilla, and I don't like strawberry."

Danielle agreed, "Me, too. Can we go somewhere else?"

Marilyn said, "Sure, I know just the place to go."

Mike put together what had just transpired with what they were talking about earlier. "Actually, what we're experiencing right now is a perfect example to show us why the explorers were willing to take the risks of exploring. They had heard of the riches of the Indies and the new world, and they wanted something else, something *more*, kind of like a person wanting different flavors of ice cream than what they've got here."

Danielle said, "You mean the explorers wanted chocolate-chip and cookie-dough ice cream?"

"Well, yeah, pretty much like that," Mike explained. Having led a weekly youth group for two years, it was easy for Mike to be patient with children.

"One of the things the explorers in the 1400s wanted to discover was a good trade route to the Indies, a faster and better way to bring back more exotic goods to the European people who couldn't otherwise afford such nice things."

"The problem had been that, to get from Portugal to the Indies, they had to travel by land," Mike continued, "through rugged mountains and dangerous terrain. It took a long time to get there and back, and there were only a limited amount of goods that they could carry."

Danielle listened with interest as Mike's enthusiasm grew. "But the explorers had a vision. Those people were 'round-earth thinkers' who were passionately committed to finding a faster route that would increase trade and improve the lives of their countrymen. They had explored enough sea routes to know that there was no valid reason to support the 'flat-earth' theory. Their strong conviction was a result of good intuition combined with experience."

Mike glanced over at Betty and his grandmother before going on, "That's what our grandmothers did, as well as all the people who made IDS a really great school. When they were working as interns or assistants with the gifted students in the public schools, they had seen that classrooms *could* be places where children could learn in a friendly, safe and positive environment. They realized classroom learning could actually be fun. Later, they developed an *idea* of a whole school where kids would be happy, where children could just be themselves and really love to learn. At the time, that was a novel idea – but they just set sail and went forward with it, committed to the journey they believed in." Mike looked satisfied with himself, as he saw that Danielle was beginning to understand.

A+ Action Approach
Leadership Lessons

> **Model the Models**
> The explorers from 500 years ago explored possibilities to achieve goals that most considered to be beyond human capabilities. Every generation breeds new models for facing, meeting and conquering new challenges.

> **Develop a Lifelong Learning Mentality**
> Training often comes in the form of stories, conversations, analogies and probing questions

that link past lessons with present experience for a potentially great future.

➤ **Persevere and Persist**
The explorers' successes were not due to a single event, but were the result of an evolutionary process that included all components of the A+ Action Approach to Leadership and Change.

The Explorers of 1968: "Two Silly Ladies"

As Marilyn drove the group to a different ice cream parlor, Mike continued, enthused by the ideas he'd been exposed to at the IDS celebration that evening. "You see," he said, focusing in on Danielle, "our grandmas took a risk in 1968. They believed that a school where kids are happy was possible, and imagined what it would be like. They talked a lot about it with each other and wrote down their dream so that they would remember it, and so that others could understand it. Then they committed to making it happen and began to take the necessary steps to begin the school. Our grandmothers got help from many sources, including parents and other teachers, and eventually, they built a team." Danielle listened intently to Mike, as they drove through the evening's light traffic.

"There were flat-earth thinkers back then who used to call them 'two silly ladies,' but our grandmas didn't care, because they had confidence that they could do it. Sometimes, when they didn't know what to do next, like the time there were too many kids and the school didn't have room for all of the students, they would take it one step at a time and ask questions of themselves like, 'What's best for the children?' and 'What do we need to do next?'

"By starting with a large plan and then breaking it down into smaller pieces, they were able to find the answers. In fact, that's how they got the land on which the school was built. Over time, other people continued to keep their dream alive. The new leaders of the school were able to do this because the dream, what they call the 'IDS philosophy,' was written down. You could say it was like a map that the explorers would use to find the new lands. You see, our grandmas were 'round-earth thinkers.' They believed in a different view of education than the flat-earth thinkers, and Independent Day School is like the ship they built to sail to a New World."

Marilyn's eyes brightened as she smiled with joyful pride, listening to her grandson's fine storytelling ability, as he described the early years of IDS.

When they pulled into the ice cream parlor's parking lot, everyone got out, entered the cheery establishment and found themselves a nice table. After placing their order with a friendly, college-aged waitress, their desserts arrived shortly. Danielle dove right into the banana split she'd been dreaming about, Johnny licked the whipped cream off the cherry before digging into his cookie-dough ice cream sundae and Mike enjoyed the taste of his pistachio scoop with nuts and fudge on top. Marilyn and Betty each sipped their old fashioned ice-cream sodas – strawberry and chocolate, respectively.

Betty turned to Michael and shared what she was thinking, "You know, there was also a lot of luck! When we graduated from our Master's program at the University of South Florida, it was the 1960s and court-ordered busing had started here in Florida. It was a time of much public unrest and uncertainty. People were afraid of what might happen in the public schools. There was enough doubt about what was going on that many were willing to try something new; so they signed up for our school."

Marilyn agreed and added, "We wanted our four children, who would be entering grades 5 through 8, to have an education that encompassed the strategies and techniques we had learned from educating gifted children." She remembered her first child, Bill. "When we were in Connecticut, he attended a school for the gifted and was encouraged to study whatever interested him the most. In second grade, his passion was dinosaurs. Soon, he was devouring everything he could find about the subject and even lectured to seventh graders about it!"

She summarized, "I saw what could come from a child's uniqueness being appreciated and attended to in a learning environment."

Marilyn slowed her pace and got quieter as she recalled, "In 1964, Bill died at sixteen in a car accident. Soon after that, we moved to Tampa. I needed something to fill the huge void in my life. A notice in the paper caught my attention about a U.S. Office of Education Fellowship program. It was 1966, and I enrolled in a special Master's program at the University of South Florida. It was the same year that my son would have started college, and that's where Betty and I met and became friends." She turned, smiled briefly at Betty, and then resumed talking about their history together.

"Our main focus was on teaching gifted children, which, in the sixties, was a "hot topic" in education. We interned at a local public school and applied the new teaching methods with elementary students who were identified as having high IQ's."

Danielle had taken an IQ test recently, so this subject piqued her interest.

"The gifted students," Marilyn paused, and then said, "you know, I've never liked that word, because I believe we all have 'gifted' strengths." She continued, "The students would be taken out of their classrooms for special work. They enjoyed the lessons so much that it made us sad to see the rest of the students missing out on such experiences. When it was time to graduate, we wanted to use what we had learned not only for our own children, but to provide a model environment where we could unlock the gifts in all children."

Betty said, "One idea we explored was to start a non-profit, private school. We were fortunate to have the support of people who worked at the University of South Florida and from some parents of our students."

Marilyn turned to see Mike more directly. "The first thing we did was write our school's philosophy, which would serve as a foundation for the school and a guide over the years in making decisions." She pulled out the award she received during the ceremony that evening and read the declaration aloud:

"IDS was founded on and remains devoted to the ideal that a happy child... one who is given respect as a unique human being and allowed to fulfill his/her needs to play, to investigate and to be him/herself... is more open to learning than a child who is unhappy, tense and fearful. We consider it our responsibility to foster each child's capacity for learning, to help him/her grow morally, spiritually, and emotionally, as well as physically and intellectually. Recognizing the many differences in learning rates and styles, we believe in individualizing each child's school experience to whatever extent is possible for the fullest development of his/her potential. It is our belief that school should be interesting and even exciting; that each child's work and behavior should be evaluated in terms of his/her own inherent capacity, rather than through comparison

with others; and that cooperation is more valuable than competition. Our goal is to provide a relaxed but stimulating atmosphere wherein each child feels acceptance and encouragement in the achievement of success through the exercise of responsible choice."

Johnny didn't understand all of the "big" words, but he could tell that they meant it was really important for kids to be happy and feel good.

Then Marilyn reached into her purse and pulled out a yellowed newspaper clipping from July 21, 1968. Handing it to Danielle, she continued "We put this ad in *The Tampa Tribune-Times*:

INDEPENDENT DAY SCHOOL
Now Considering Applications for School Year
1968-'69
A New Middle School for Grades **5 - 8**
INTERFAITH and INTERRACIAL
Interested Parents Are Invited . . .
OPEN HOUSE – TUESDAY!
July 23, 1968, 7 to 9 p.m., Room 11
At TEMPLE TERRACE PRESBYTERIAN CHURCH
420 Bullard Parkway
Mrs. W. Gatlin Mrs. J. Anderson

"We received such a strong response from the ad that we were able to lease six classrooms on the second floor of the Temple Terrace Presbyterian Church. We felt it was important that the new school be open to students of all faiths and color, an emerging issue in those times. As it turned out, thirty students enrolled the first year in grades 5 through 8. It was very exciting! Betty and I taught some of the classes, and we hired USF grad students to teach the rest. The second year, at the request of parents, we started expanding to include the younger grades by adding a fourth grade. By the third year, kindergarten through third grades were added, with a total of 80 students enrolled. Now we were running out of space!"

"It was challenging, but we always knew it would work out." Marilyn turned to Michael and said with a knowing smile, "We had our fair share of leadership challenges. Some of these included: attempting to relate well with people in the community who often saw us as "just a hippie school," figuring out how to organize and systematize what we were doing, and setting aside enough time to figure out how or where we were going to get enough funds raised to continue running the school." She breathed a deep sigh and rolled her eyes over toward Betty, as though recalling some of the difficult times they shared in the past.

Looking back to her young audience, she continued, "A few months earlier, Michael, your grandfather had found an 8-acre property with peacocks strolling everywhere and a pond right in the middle of it; but the two spinster sisters who lived on the property told him that it was 'absolutely not' for sale. Your grandfather had fallen in love with the land, and I eventually convinced him that we should talk to them again. I told the sisters about our students, who needed a school, but did not have a place to go. As it turned out, they were retired teachers. By the time I finished talking, one sister turned to the other and said, 'Now, we can't let these children not have a place to go to school, can we?' The other sister replied, 'No, I guess we can't.' And that's how the land was purchased." She smiled, remembering that day with a particular fondness.

"The classrooms had to be built quickly, and we wanted them to last. We ended up with five round buildings that provided *a relaxed, but stimulating atmosphere.* It seemed like a miracle that they were ready for the opening of school in September!"

"The next year, Betty and I were both feeling the stress of teaching and leading the school, which was growing so fast. We decided it was a good time to find a new headmaster."

"Jim Bradley took over as headmaster and quickly started developing the first Board of Trustees. He supervised the construction of a geodesic dome. The Dome became the classroom for the middle school students, who proudly called themselves 'Domies.' This building, based on structural designs by Buckminster Fuller, made local news and the school became known for its unique landmark."

Mike and Danielle smiled at the name. "Domies," Mike repeated and Danielle grinned in response. Marilyn smiled, too, as she recounted IDS' pioneering days. "Up until this time, students were not given traditional report cards with letter grades. Our school was seeking every way possible to embrace each child's uniqueness, so each teacher wrote handwritten letters describing the students' behavior, attention span, comprehension level and how well they cooperated with fellow students. The teachers really got to know each student, and worked hard to help them develop their strengths."

Danielle imagined aloud, as a 12-year old might, "No grades…I wonder what *that* would be like! My best friend gets into so much trouble with some of the grades she gets. I bet her life would be a lot easier and happier with *that* kind of report card!"

Marilyn nodded. "Well, it sounds good," she agreed, "but it was hard to manage. When Jim Bradley became headmaster, he had the teachers include letter grades, too. He realized that we needed more structure in the very free environment that we had created. Jim brought balance to the school through his ability to integrate freedom and structure. This is something that every one of our school leaders has sought to maintain." She smiled thinking about all of Jim's contributions to IDS.

By then, the five-some had finished their dessert and Johnny was fighting off sleep. Mike, however, wanted to hear more of Marilyn and Betty's story. He knew about their first years at the school, but did not know much about it after that. He was especially curious, because he was writing a research paper on leadership and change and had decided to use IDS for his study, inspired by his grandmother's accomplishments. ·

***

To help him gather the most accurate information, Marilyn had arranged a breakfast meeting for Mike to interview Cornelia Corbett. Cornelia was an IDS parent who was recognized for her outstanding leadership for more than twenty years as an IDS Board member, president and philanthropist. Pam Ripple, the current Associate Headmaster, was also invited to attend because her 25-year tenure at IDS and her unique ability to retain details naturally established her as the school's living historian. Danielle, too, was interested in being part of the meeting, since she wanted to learn more about what her grandmother had achieved in her younger days, especially at IDS.

The hour was getting late as they drove to Marilyn's house, where Betty and the children were spending the night. Mike thought about the next morning's interview, as he walked Johnny to his bed in the guestroom before heading off to sleep. Mike had already spoken with Pam Ripple and knew that, in 2002, the Board of Trustees had announced their unanimous decision to rename Independent Day School. It was now to be Independent Day School: Corbett Campus. He learned that Cornelia Corbett, her husband Richard, and her family's foundation,

The William Stamps Farish Fund, had generously donated to the school for years.

Cornelia was known around IDS as a "doer." When the school needed new classrooms and buildings because the old ones were unsafe, she would take action to see that these became a reality by making substantial donations, while motivating and challenging the community to match her gifts. Mike really wanted to know what made IDS so special to Cornelia, as well as what would motivate someone to continue to dedicate her life to support a school, even after her children had graduated.

A+ Action Approach
Leadership Lessons

> **Embrace a Vision**
> The leaders sustained a compelling idea that held enough power and possibility that they were willing to proceed.

> **Proceed Purposefully**
> Right from the start, the words in the IDS philosophy captured the big ideas and served as a beacon to light the way. Leaders created a plan delineating the details that could bring the philosophy to life.
> Risk-taking, courage, creative thinking and option-seeking permeated the leaders' actions.

> **Build Leadership Capacity, Teams and Networks**
> Multiple sources of support emerged through networking with like-minded people (in this

instance, university contacts, parents and a
partnership in leadership).

Putting Kids First

It was a gorgeous Saturday morning, worthy of
spending time outdoors – cool enough to provide a
delicious breeze, but warm enough to be comfortable in a
light jacket. The sun was shining at 9 a.m. when Cornelia
Corbett, affectionately known as "Cornie," called Mike and
suggested they meet at the school's courtyard. Mike asked
Cornie if she would mind having Danielle join in on their
conversation, and was glad when Cornie said that it would
be fine.

Betty and Johnny were still asleep, but Marilyn decided
to come along and stay for a while to enjoy the walk down
memory lane. She liked to spend time on the school
grounds, especially on days like this.

They arrived a couple of minutes early and were quietly
enjoying the light breeze, when Cornie pulled up in a black
Jeep Cherokee. As his "interviewee" emerged from her car,
Mike observed that she was a casually dressed woman with
a slight build, stylish short hair and twinkling eyes.

"Good morning," Cornie called to the threesome.

"Why don't we walk over to the picnic tables by the
pond; there's a beautiful view," Marilyn suggested.

"Sure," Mike said with a bright smile. "Thanks for
meeting us today, Mrs. Corbett."

Danielle smiled slightly. She was unusually quiet this
morning.

When they were seated, Cornie looked at Mike and
smiled, "Please call me Cornie." She addressed her new

friend, "I understand that you're studying leadership development in college and that you're writing a paper about IDS."

"Yes," Mike replied, "I'm really impressed by what's been accomplished here in the past 35 years. Not only has IDS grown to more than 500 students, but from what my grandmother tells me, the reason the school is enjoying its success today is because addressing the unique needs of each student continues to be its main priority."

"Yes," Cornie said with a big smile, "it's really great to see, isn't it?"

Cornie turned to Danielle and said, "Before Mike gets underway with his interview, I want to invite you to ask or bring up anything that's on *your* mind, as well."

The bright eighth grader smiled widely and said, "Well, my social studies class is learning about family roots and genealogy, and, I'd like to learn more about Grandma Betty's history." Danielle believed that most adults didn't care much for what twelve-year olds had to say, so she really appreciated how attentive Cornie was as they spoke. She felt very important and proud to be included during Mike's interviews.

"It's a history of which you both can be proud," Cornie replied. "Dr. Swarzman and Ms. Ripple will be joining us later, so be sure to save some questions for them."

Mike began, "What made IDS so special to you that you would dedicate so much of your life to the school?"

Cornie paused for a moment, looking at the pond, which glistened in the morning light. "In 1978, my family moved from New York to Tampa. My eldest daughter, who was in first grade, loved school in New York, but did *not* have a good experience in the first private school I sent her to. When we moved, she was unhappy and stressed, and got carsick every morning on her way to school."

Cornie reflected about how much she had learned since then. "I didn't want to move her from that school mid-year, because I wanted to teach her the importance of finishing what you start – had I known then what I know now, I would have moved her immediately." She raised her eyebrows and rolled her eyes a little as she gave them a knowing glance.

She continued, "In the spring of 1980, I began searching for a new school for her. When I visited IDS, the headmaster and the staff of teachers assured me that every effort was made to teach students according to their learning style and their readiness level."

Mike asked, "Did they reassure you that would happen for *your* daughter?"

"They told me that all students were respected in the classroom and *allowed to fulfill their needs to play, to investigate and to be themselves.* I realized, from what I saw, that this could be a great place for my children."

Cornie pulled out the Program from the celebration and pointed to the following sentences in the IDS philosophy as she read it aloud, *"IDS was founded on and remains devoted to the ideal that a happy child – one who is given respect as a unique human being and allowed to fulfill his needs to play, to investigate and to be himself – is more open to learning..."*

Danielle read along, too. Mike felt impressed by the philosophy, and was beginning to understand its significance.

Cornie continued, "We moved our daughter to IDS in second grade and enrolled my other three children in the school when they were of age. Lessons were based on unique needs and developmental readiness. At IDS, rather than forcing them to learn lessons according to their chronological age, their lessons were based on what they were ready to learn."

She smiled at the two young people as they sat listening to her share her story.

"Some children learn creatively, some analytically, some are fast learners and some need more time to digest new information. My children all found their own strengths and interests, and their teachers gave them the support they needed to bring out their best. Today, they all have a passion for learning and are not afraid to take risks." There was a sense of humble satisfaction in her voice as she spoke of her children, and Mike could tell she was proud of them.

"You see, the merit of a philosophy or an idea ought to be found in the results it produces. My eldest daughter started feeling better in the mornings before school when she began attending IDS, and I saw firsthand what could happen at a school like this. My kids would literally jump out of the car and head straight for their classes, excitedly yelling, 'Bye, Mom!'"

She grinned at the memory, and then went on, "The teachers here don't just talk about the IDS philosophy, they bring it to life. They demonstrate a love of children, skill at teaching and share a vision of classroom education that includes every child rising to his or her own full potential." She paused, and then added, "And when Dr. Swarzman came onboard as headmaster with her emphasis on weekly staff training and using a research-based approach to learning, the teachers began to get even better. But I'm sure you'll be hearing more about that when you talk with her."

Danielle wished that all kids could go to a school like IDS. She started to imagine what her life would be like if she had that opportunity in her home state of North Carolina.

Mike interrupted Danielle's thoughts, "Wow, Cornie, it sounds like you love the school because of how much it gave your children."

"That's true, I do love the school because of what it did for my kids, *and* I wanted more kids to be able to have the opportunity to receive this kind of education." She paused, "I still do. All kids should be happy about going to school and excited about learning."

"I agree, Cornie!" Mike exclaimed.

A+ Action Approach
Leadership Lessons

➤ **Model the Models**
Seek out the "role models" that exist within most organizations. Tap into leadership and "concretize"* the secrets that led them to success.

➤ **Embrace a Vision**
Tell your "story" as often as possible to reinforce the message and enthusiastically spread the energy generated from a worthy vision.

* Definition of *concretize*:
Take an idea and make it concrete.
Identify common characteristics that can be replicated over time.

Finding the Right Leaders

Cornie looked up and smiled as she noticed Pam Ripple walking toward them.

"Good morning, Pam," they all said, welcoming her to join in on the conversation.

"Hi, everyone," Pam said kindly as she sat down at the picnic bench with Mike, Danielle, Marilyn and Cornie. Pam's warm smile and soothing personality radiated through her deep blue eyes. "Go ahead with what you were doing. I'm going to listen."

As Pam settled herself into the group, Mike cleared his throat and took the lead. "Well, I was just about to ask Cornie about her leadership experience at IDS." Mike turned to Cornie, "How did you first get involved with the Board of Trustees?"

"In 1980," Cornie replied, "I was a parent volunteer, and soon joined the Board of Trustees. The teachers or the administration would have needs, and we would try to help them. In 1981, I was elected President of the Board."

Looking at the list of questions in his notebook, Mike asked, "What were some of the challenges you and the Board faced?"

"Change was the biggest challenge in our past," Cornie responded, "and we certainly had our fair share! The task of maintaining forward progress and group harmony when dealing with a large and diverse group of people required not only profound knowledge and skill, but also a healthy balance of both determination and flexibility. We developed a tenacious sense of perseverance *and* a yielding sense of adaptability! One challenge we repeatedly faced was deciding on the leadership of the school." Cornie looked over at Pam with a sense that the two of them had sailed many seas together. Pam nodded knowingly about the fact that IDS had had nine headmasters in 35 years.

"We hit a couple of bumps in the road," Cornie reminisced, "but each person always seemed to bring something to the school that was needed at the time."

"With each headmaster, we raised our standards; we became more organized and effective in meeting the needs of the school, and, more importantly, at better serving our students."

Pam added, "Cornie, why don't you tell Mike about the key periods in the history of IDS's leadership that really catapulted the school forward with passion."

"Great idea," Cornie replied. "First, of course, there were Marilyn and Betty. They gave the school its foundation. Dr. Gatlin, Marilyn's former husband, and a few key parents supported and guided the school in its early beginnings," she said.

Cornie looked over at Marilyn, who chimed in, "That's right. It was the support of people who believed in our school that kept us going. Looking back, it's funny, but sometimes I didn't know if I would get a paycheck at the end of the week...and neither did some of the teachers. Thank goodness that's all changed now!"

"Our early group of teachers and IDS supporters kept the philosophy alive with their insight, devotion, and heartfelt determination to see it happen," Marilyn explained.

They all turned to see a brightly colored peacock strut past, fluttering its feathers.

"Then there was Jim Bradley," Cornie continued. "He came right after Marilyn and Betty, and was here from 1970 to 1974. That was before my family came to IDS." She turned to Marilyn and asked, "How did Jim's leadership impact the school?"

"Jim Bradley brought a sense of how to set things up," Marilyn replied, "He implemented better systems for organization and accountability, so that decisions could be made based on a well-defined administrative structure. During that period in IDS history, we were beginning to see our heartfelt, child-centered school grow into a bigger, more structured community. And certainly one of our challenges, as IDS grew, was to continue to preserve the tender feelings and bonds of family we'd felt as a smaller school."

"A third key period," Pam shared, as she looked over towards Mike, "was in the 1980s, when Dr. Bernie Haake was headmaster. That was about a year after Cornie joined us. Bernie had been a public school superintendent, and also spent time in a cabinet position in the state of New York. He was a forward-thinking, innovative educator and administrator. I remember the first time he visited us. It was the last day of school and we were giving out awards to every child in the school, whether it was for the happiest smile, best attendance or highest grades. Bernie said, 'I want to be part of a school where every child is recognized.'"

"For seven years, Bernie helped us raise our standards of excellence in a much bigger way than ever before. He prioritized reading and writing programs, as well as the development of early childhood education, because he strongly recognized the importance of the early years. It was under his leadership that planning began for new construction for our growing school. That was such a neat experience because he and the architect included both the kids and the teachers to help create actual models for how they dreamed the school would be designed." Pam looked over at Cornie, who knew how much admiration Pam had for Bernie and what he'd done for the school.

Cornie chimed in, "That's part of our hands-on philosophy here at IDS. We involve the students in many of the important changes that we make, especially those that affect them directly. The older students," she went on, "actually helped give input into the design of our new middle school. The young teens chose a silver-gray color for the building because they wanted to have a more grown-up and high-tech image. It gave them a sense of ownership."

Cornie reflected for a moment about the main message she wanted to convey to Mike and Danielle. "As every situation arose, we would always go back to the philosophy and ask the question, 'What's best for the children?' It always comes down to that."

Pam nodded to Cornie, encouraging her to continue. "And our fourth, most recent, key period began in 1996, when we hired Dr. Joyce Burick Swarzman. She had gained an incredible reputation for her leadership in education; and, at that time, had been heading an honors program for education majors at the University of South Florida College of Education for fifteen years."

"What happened between the time Bernie left and Joyce joined IDS?" Mike asked.

"Well, for one reason or another," Pam answered, "we moved from one headmaster to another. They each had their strengths, and that's how we like to remember them. At IDS, we're committed to living our philosophy; we have high ideals, and it takes a very special person to lead this school." She paused for a moment, reflecting about what to say next.

"In 1996," she explained, "when we were searching for a new headmaster and invited Joyce to take that position, she was at a great time in her career and we didn't know if she would want the position. Most people go from leading a school to teaching at a university, not the other way around! But Joyce was intrigued by the idea."

Cornie said, "She liked our passion and believed in our vision. I think she also wanted the challenge of putting her university principles into practice. I'd tease her sometimes about that. I'd stop by her office and say, 'So how are your theories now, Joyce?' and she would laugh!"

"Hiring Joyce," Cornie added, "was unusual because she had no experience in leading a private school. In the past, we had always hired people by asking for their resumes. This time, the resume didn't fit, but the person did."

Pam laughed, "I remember when Joyce told me about how she made her decision. She said that her brain would say, 'This is not a good idea. Why would you ever want to leave the university?' But at the same time, her gut and intuition would push her, 'Do it. This is where you need to be; this is the right thing to do now!' We all know which, in the end, she trusted more!"

Cornie jumped in, "During each period of leadership, what so often helped us was the dedication of the members of the Board of Trustees… and of people like Pam Ripple," she gestured to Pam, "who helped keep the school together through its many changes."

"Thanks, Cornie. Living our philosophy is always what has made the difference," said Pam. "That's what makes this school feel so magical. For example, Jim Conlin, our current Board president, says that he enrolled his two girls at IDS because of the incredibly positive feeling he got when he visited our grounds. That was about eight years ago. Always believing in the kids and in the uniqueness of each child--that's what motivates all of us to keep growing, and that's what makes education come alive here."

Pam recalled the Board's commitment even back in the early days. "I remember a time when we were having difficulty making payroll for salaries. The Board members took a risk and signed a personal note, because they believed so deeply in how the school was helping the children."

Cornie thought for a moment, remembering those days and then shared, "Our accounting system was updated, thanks to Bruce Davies, a dedicated Board member who led the finance committee and helped make the school financially stable by creating an accounting system that was more manageable. He was supported by our business manager, JoAnne Mason. You may be wondering what this has to do with the kids. Well, with the new system in place, the headmaster could make wiser and more efficient decisions regarding financial matters. It was all part of the evolution of a growing school."

Mike took notes as quickly as he could, and after he caught up, looked at Cornie with a newly discovered respect and awe for her accomplishments. "I can see that you and the Board have done a great job at strengthening IDS' ability to keep its ideals alive. How did you develop *your* leadership abilities?"

"It's what we all did," she replied. "Everyone pitched in to make it work. For me, personally, I wanted to be an effective leader; so I attended educational workshops. I particularly benefited from the ones I attended with the Florida Council for Independent Schools and with Independent School Management. I learned how to be a Chairman of a Board, how to structure committees, how to run a meeting, how to do evaluations and much more. Then, I would come back and teach the Board members what I learned. I always enjoyed looking for a new forum, a new idea, to keep it fresh."

Mike recognized, as Cornie spoke, that she carried herself naturally and unassumingly as a leader, adopting a presence of both strength and humility. "I also shared my vision with the Board that IDS would become an example of what education could be for every child." Cornie's voice rose as she exclaimed, "They're happy and they want to learn. Why can't every school be this way? Why is there drudgery? Why is there humiliation? Why is there fear? It's so unnecessary. Kids learn better when there is *none* of that."

Mike was surprised by her sudden burst of passion. He was pleased to know someone who understood children as well as she did. Then he asked her, "Do you think that all schools, both public and private, can apply what IDS does?"

"Absolutely!" Cornie responded. "It's all in the teacher training, and that's the current period we're in. Initially, we had people who intuitively knew how to relate to kids. Little did I know that in just a few years, with the arrival of Dr. Swarzman, IDS would begin its own teacher training program that would result in a more systematic approach to create positive learning environments that are now being observed by hundreds of well-respected educators, from both the public and private sectors. We've even begun a fellowship and residency program, where new teachers and potential teachers stay with us for a year to learn our methods and have the opportunity to be mentored by *our* teachers."

Mike was fascinated by the profound role mentoring can play in human potential and motivation. He was particularly interested in how people's early experiences with role models would influence their behavior later in life.

"Cornie, I would imagine that the school's leaders, having been as diverse as you've described them, derived their strengths from a wide variety of role models. Who or what was your guiding influence in shaping who you are as a leader? Did you have someone who taught you the ropes, aside from the training classes you took?"

"There was no one who taught me what to do *exactly...*" Cornie's gaze shifted to the tops of the trees as she recalled, "When I was a young girl, my grandmother would always come up north from Houston, Texas, to visit with the family. One time, she called my mother to tell her that she would be late by about two or three days because she said that she had an appointment. My mom later found out that Grandmother's 'appointment' was a banquet where she was honored with the Annual Philanthropic Award from the entire city of Houston." She thought for a moment, and then said, "It pleased my grandmother, a very humble woman, to make a difference, quietly and behind the scenes."

"Wow..." Mike said. He felt like he had just been given a gem. He had heard at the 35th year celebration that people followed Cornie by her example, and realized that her style of leadership emanated from her own grandmother's modeling.

Mike said, "Grandma Marilyn told me that you were also a leader when you were in school."

"That's true," Cornie replied. "I captained the ninth grade girls' sports teams. We would rotate sports every season and I enjoyed all of them. I practiced a lot."

Danielle was listening attentively, keenly noticing the parallels between Cornie's childhood memories and her current successes. The idea of creating positive and powerful experiences while she was still young was dawning on her youthful mind.

Footsteps could be heard on the wooden walkway at the rear of the school. Everyone turned around to see Dr. Joyce Swarzman approaching with a white three-ring binder in one arm and a medium-sized brown bag in the other. Mike hoped it was a snack; he was getting a little hungry. Two peacocks stood by a low cement wall behind Joyce, one proudly fanning his feathers.

"Hello," she called to the group. "Are you having a good time?"

They all smiled and greeted Joyce, a slender, brunette woman with an infectious smile and dynamic energy. Danielle and Mike both nodded enthusiastically, and simultaneously said, "Yes."

"Thanks, Cornie and Pam, for visiting with Mike and Danielle today," Joyce said with gratitude. "It's a nice surprise to see you too, Marilyn. I just stopped by to say 'hello' and see how you're doing. I'm meeting with a family in a few minutes, so I'll see you in a little while."

"Speaking of family,' Joyce added, "Pam, make sure you tell them what the teachers said about our school." As she placed a bag of bagels and juice on the table, Joyce said to everyone, "Here's a little something for you, in case you're hungry."

"Thanks, Joyce, your timing is perfect," said Mike.

Before Joyce walked back to the office, Pam turned to Mike and Danielle and said, "Joyce is talking about a video and interviews that we did with all of the teachers and staff. One of the questions was, 'What feeling do you get when you think of IDS?' Every teacher had good things to share, but what surprised us the most was that almost every one of them used the words 'family' or 'home' to describe their feeling here."

Proudly, Joyce added, "Even visitors from outside of IDS seem to catch the spirit. For example, when Pam Simms, the author of the award-winning educational bestseller, *Awakening Brilliance*, came to our school, she raved about us. Her exact words were, 'Visiting IDS was like walking into my book. I actually saw my book come to life for the first time.'"

Cornie grinned at Joyce's remarks, as Joyce turned to face the group, gave a thumbs-up and departed for the office.

A+ Action Approach
Leadership Lessons

➤ **Model the Models**
Behind every great or growing leader is one or several mentors who influence the formation of his or her character and deeds. Recognizing the gifts of mentors serves to reinforce the admired behaviors and/or showcase past profound experiences that help sustain their positive influence.

➤ **Adopt a Presence**
Leadership excellence is demonstrated in word and action, as well as the attitude one carries and conveys. The light of true leadership naturally emanates from those who are genuinely inspired by a commitment to service.

➤ **Develop a Lifelong Learning Mentality**
In all areas of an organization, "Training! Training! Training!" is key. Deliberately carving out the time is necessary to accomplish that.

➤ **Build Leadership Capacity**
Keep going until you find the right leadership. Don't settle. When you find someone extraordinary, do all you can to keep him or her. Build a culture that recognizes the advantages of longevity.

The Root of a Happy Child

The time was passing quickly, so Cornie continued to share with her guests. "It's difficult to describe the feeling that many people get when they visit IDS. Some people say that it's 'magical.' The strong family feeling that the teachers describe is what makes our school so special. Every one of our teachers is absolutely committed to caring about every child, and each one does whatever it takes to help every child learn. The teachers work together as a team. They are the heroes, the ones who really bring the philosophy to life for our students." Mike noticed that Cornie's words carried a sentiment of deep appreciation.

"You see, no matter how big we get," she said, "there is still that connection between the teacher and the child, and that is the very root of the happy child."

"The challenge is," Cornie added, "how to keep that feeling in a growing school, so that no matter how big we get, the intimacy between the teachers and the kids is still alive."

Danielle could tell that Cornie had great admiration for what the teachers had accomplished at IDS, and wished that all kids could have such a wonderful experience. She wondered out loud, "Is that why you're still here, Cornie, even though your children have already graduated?"

"Yes. But I'm not the only one. There are others who have remained active members of the Board for *years* after their children have graduated. It's easy to stay at a place where it feels like family, and where such a positive difference for so many kids is being made. And by the way, there are *teachers*, too, who have stayed long after their own children have graduated from IDS."

Cornie suggested to Mike, "Why don't you take a few moments to think about what you've heard so far about IDS and see if any of this is helpful to you in writing your paper on leadership. Meanwhile, let's eat!"

***

Mike was grateful for the break, so that he could reflect on what he'd learned and remember it. Wanting to retain as much as he could, he turned the page of his notebook and summarized his notes about Marilyn, Betty, Cornie and Pam by describing the leadership qualities of all four women:

- Open-minded
- Committed
- Lead by example
- Persistent
- Dedicated
- Passionate
- Risk-takers
- Good communicators
- Kind
- Proud

He noted that each of these leaders turned to the IDS philosophy or her own ideal values for answers and, when faced with a challenge, would ask the question, "What is best for the child?" Like great leaders in any field, these women demonstrated their commitment to the people they served by doing whatever it took to find a solution and following through until it was achieved. Mike saw that Marilyn, Betty, Cornie and Pam had purposefully persevered to keep the tender, vital connection between each student and his or her teachers both strong and vibrant. He wondered what Dr. Swarzman's contributions to IDS were and looked forward to hearing her story.

Meanwhile, Danielle had walked slowly over to the peacock, but could only get within 6 feet before he flew off. She sat down on the cement wall and thought about the contributions of Marilyn, Grandma Betty, Pam and Cornie.

"Marilyn is a fun storyteller," she mused to herself. "She's outgoing and full of ideas. Grandma Betty is more practical and realistic, but will stand behind something she believes in, even if it seems impossible. Pam was there for more than twenty years, through all of the changes, helping to keep IDS a happy place for all the kids and teachers, just like our grandmas wanted when they started the school. And Cornie…hmm…," Danielle reflected for a moment. "…Cornie and the Board have kept our grandmas' dream alive by finding the right people to lead the school and making sure that there's enough money to keep it going!" She smiled, enjoying her "ah-ha" moment and feeling tremendous family pride.

A+ Action Approach
Leadership Lessons

➢ **Embrace the Vision**
Telling your story brings insight and greater clarity of purpose.

A Supportive Board Lives the Philosophy

After sharing a light brunch of bagels, cream cheese and orange juice, Mike eagerly jumped right into his first question. "You mentioned teamwork, Cornie, when you spoke about the teachers. What is the teamwork like on the Board?"

Cornie was thoughtful for a moment before she replied, "Well, back to the philosophy, the most important question we ask ourselves is-…"

"…What's best for the kids?" Mike and Danielle completed her sentence.

"That's right! To be a successful team, we've got to have strong communication with the school leaders. For example, our headmasters are an important part of our Board meetings. They let us know what the teachers and students need, and keep us aware of issues that affect the school and policies that the Board oversees. When Joyce is making a decision about something important, she knows she can turn to us anytime. She and I, as well as the current Board President, have a very good relationship, where we bounce things off of each other whenever we want to. I guess the most important thing is that once we choose a leader, we give him or her our full support."

Facing Danielle, she added, "I remember just before we found Joyce. We knew we wanted to do something new and different. We'd always had a good school. We wanted someone who could make it *soar!*"

Cornie glanced briefly at Pam, "As I mentioned earlier, leadership in education is more than simply having knowledge of the field. True leadership at a school requires an open-mindedness to constantly improve. As Joyce is fond of saying, "a life-long learning mentality." With Joyce's training background and her passion for discovering the 'New World' of education, we believed she was the right one."

Danielle encouraged Cornie, "Tell us more about Joyce."

"In the beginning of her career," Cornie responded, "she taught in the inner cities of Chicago, Atlanta and New York. She prides herself on that, because her students liked being in her classes and would show up to class every day.

Later, she became a teacher-trainer and faculty member at the University of South Florida (USF), the same school that your grandmothers attended."

Pam added, "That's where she devoted fifteen years to the SunCoast Area Teacher Training (SCATT)* program, which began as an honors program to attract and keep bright and talented students in education. She would train both pre-service and outstanding in-service teachers in the latest strategies to bring out the best in their students. For years, she also trained statewide 'Teacher Of The Year' award winners." Danielle quickly thought about some of the teachers that she'd had who'd inspired her to do her best.

They all turned to see Joyce approaching them. "Are you talking about me?" she asked, beaming her usual good-natured grin.

*SCATT is the SUNCOAST AREA TEACHER TRAINING HONORS PROGRAM. Dr. Joyce Swarzman served as a director of SCATT, was the Associate Director of Clinical Education at the University of South Florida's College of Education and also the Associate Director of the David C. Anchin Center for the Advancement of Teaching. Under her leadership, the SCATT program's reputation for excellence in teacher training soared, as Dr. Swarzman trained more than 10,000 teachers and education students in leading edge communication and teaching skills. SCATT received national acclaim in 1985 when the American Association of State Colleges and Universities Showcase for Excellence Award was presented to SCATT for outstanding accomplishments with talented students in education. SCATT was also recognized as one of the most innovative teacher training programs in the country. For more than twenty years, principals have continued to seek out SCATT graduates, because they are known as being highly skilled, innovative and prepared to go the extra mile.

A+ Action Approach
Leadership Lessons

> **Build Leadership Capacity, Teams and Networks**
> A hierarchy that thrives on communication becomes more like a bridge than a ladder. Open, respectful and frequent communication throughout an organization encourages a dynamic synergy among the members.

The Makings of a Leader

Marilyn, who was quietly listening and enjoying the conversation, answered, "As a matter of fact, yes, we were talking about you. I keep telling Mike that you're one of the best things that has happened to IDS, Joyce! Pam and Cornie were just telling us about some of the things you did before you joined the IDS family."

Mike eagerly piped in, "Joyce, what are your earliest memories of being a leader?"

Joyce looked around to make sure she had everyone's total attention; then she exclaimed, "'Joyce Burick, I will be so happy when you move!' Those were the real words from my sixth grade teacher, Mrs. Geiger, as she grabbed her big black purse and went crying out of the classroom."

Joyce enjoyed the surprised expressions on everyone's faces, except for Cornie and Pam, who already knew this story. They just smiled quietly.

"I don't even remember what awful thing I got the class to chant to the teacher; but before I knew it, the whole class was standing on their nailed-to-the-ground desks and shouting right along with me."

Mike couldn't help but laugh, but he winced thinking about the humiliation that the teacher must have felt.

As he and Danielle looked at Joyce with astonishment, she said, "You might be asking yourself how a sixth-grade class clown and trouble maker, strong enough to create a mob-scene in a classroom, could become the headmaster of a school?"

The mood of the group sobered as Joyce made her point. "You see," she began, "as we all stood on our desks chanting, I had very mixed feelings. At the same time that I felt the exhilaration of power with everybody following my lead, I also felt a tremendous sick feeling in my stomach for the pain that I'd caused my teacher. I remember thinking, 'Oh my goodness, what have I done?' Because of that experience, I truly understand the importance of leading children with firm guidance, as well as with heart. While children should have the power of choice, it should only be wielded in a way that is respectful and sensitive to others."

Danielle recognized her mother's words about giving children limited choices and about being kind, as well as firm. Even though Danielle didn't enjoy it when her mother used that strategy on her, she admitted to herself that it made her feel safe, in a strange kind of way.

"What were your first years like at IDS, Joyce?" asked Mike.

"Coming here was very different than I thought it would be. When I accepted a two-year contract with IDS, I saw it as a great opportunity to *walk the talk* and put into practice the very points I had been teaching and training for so many years. I naively thought I could change the world in two years, then return to the university with field experience that would make my work there even better." She laughed, "That was seven years ago!"

Joyce stopped a moment and looked out in the direction of the pond. "It takes time for changes to take hold and I faced a lot of challenges. One of my mentors at USF, Bill Katzenmeyer, the former Dean of the College of Education, helped me during my first years at IDS. He understood my vision. His leadership, skill and firm grasp of what I was trying to accomplish at IDS gave me the confidence and guidance to move forward, especially when I faced the tough challenges that often come with change."

It surprised Mike to hear Joyce say that she needed someone to give her confidence. She seemed so self-assured. But he was beginning to realize that the road to leadership excellence is often a challenging one, even for people who have experience and confidence.

A+ Action Approach
Leadership Lessons

➤ **Model the Models**
At every juncture of one's career, seeking advice is required from time to time. You'd have to be a fool to try and do it on your own!

Four Golden Rules to Hire and Keep the Best Staff

Mike and Danielle were given a more candid view of Joyce when she shared, "During March of 1996, before my arrival as headmaster, I was scheduled to meet with the IDS faculty for the first time. The meeting was to be held at 3:15 p.m. When I walked in, there were couches and furniture strewn everywhere; it was a hodge-podge! Then, Don Dewey, one of the teachers, firmly and authoritatively told me, 'I just wanted you to know that we leave at 3:30.'"

"At that moment, I knew that my work was cut out for me. Actually, the first thing I did was to get rid of that furniture and set up a training room!" She smiled at the recollection, then turned toward Mike and continued. "I also knew that if we were going to grow to be a staff that is always learning and develop into a real learning community, then, as long as I was here, we'd need to meet from 3:30 to 5:00 p.m. every Tuesday to sharpen our skills and improve our abilities."

Pam added, "That marked the beginning of a new era, and not everyone liked it. Within two-and-a-half years, a lot of the staff turned over."

Mike knew what a challenge it was when people left their jobs. New people had to be hired and trained, and fast! That could take up a lot of an organization's time and waste valuable resources, if it wasn't put in check. "Tell me more about the changes with the staff. How did you handle all of that?" he asked.

Joyce thought for a moment as they watched three peacocks stroll by.

"From my mentors, I learned four golden rules to hiring and keeping the best staff." She raised one finger at a time, as she made each point.

"One, find the best faculty – teachers who are both competent and caring. That means teachers who enjoy children and who are also committed to being lifelong learners.

"Two, empower them to make things happen.

"Three, provide the very best ongoing training to support them in getting the job done.

"And four, treat teachers as professionals by setting high expectations for excellence."

After a pause, she added, "A commitment to professional development and continuous study is probably one of my greatest contributions to IDS. The staff and I have worked together to create a standard of excellence together from which we can all reach and grow."

"There were many USF College of Education SCATT teachers and graduates who caught the vision of what was happening at IDS. This made my job a little bit easier, because they understood the meaning of high expectations already and were used to going the extra mile. The SCATT program prided itself in emphasizing the 'above-and-beyond' mentality."

Joyce stood up and looked over at Mike. "It also helped that we created a team effort among our administrators." Pam and Joyce smiled as they thought about their office's version of the 'Steel Magnolias,' led by the business manager, Mrs. Mason, and the Director of Advancement, Mrs. Barfield.

"Pam became my greatest ally and support," Joyce said as she glanced over at her with admiration and gratitude. "I could tell her or ask her anything, and she would help me get through it, whether she agreed or not! She is a tremendous resource to this school because she's been here for more than twenty years – first as a teacher, then as an administrator. In the beginning, I would also turn to her and ask, 'What's the history?' as I tried to discern the school's 'sacred cows,' referring to its traditions. Her advice was always invaluable. She lives the IDS philosophy." Pam looked a little uncomfortable; she never liked it when Joyce put the spotlight on her.

"Thanks, Joyce," Pam replied, "Are you ready to show Mike and Danielle the IDS *M.O.R.E. Approach*, the bag of options that every teacher here has?"

Mike looked admiringly toward Joyce, realizing that she was a leader who, indeed, "walked the talk." He saw this in her commitment to the "Olympic mentality"—the best getting better—and in her dedication to bringing on board those people who met the high standards of excellence she'd just recounted for the group. *"Any school could have this!"* he thought. *"They just need leadership that's truly committed to taking the steps to turn this vision into reality."* Mike was beginning to get a sense of clarity and excitement about what schools could become.

A+ Action Approach
Leadership Lessons

➤ **Build Leadership Capacity, Teams and Networks**
In every organization:
- Identify your allies... people who you can trust, people who will listen, and people who have the courage to tell you the truth, whether they agree with you or not.
- Have the confidence to surround yourself with strong people.
- Identify the best people and find ways to give them what they need to get the job done.

- Seek competent and caring individuals when building teams and networks.

➤ **Persevere and Persist**
Set high expectations and have the courage to stand by them.

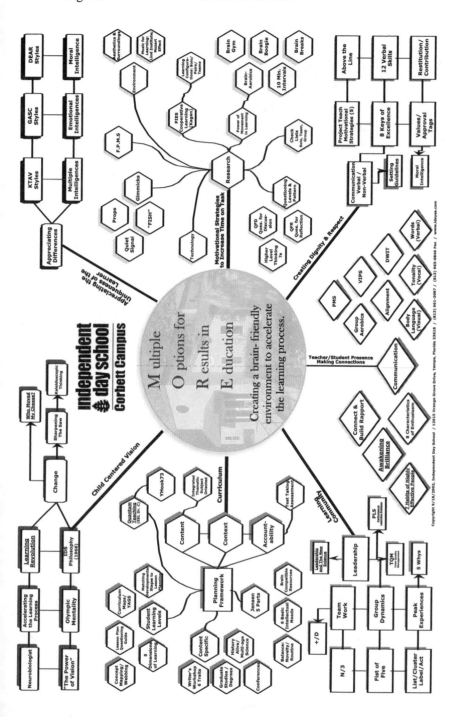

Training Makes a Difference: *The M.O.R.E. Approach*

Joyce pulled out a two-page booklet of the IDS *M.O.R.E. Approach* and opened it up to the middle, revealing a huge "mind-map." She turned it so that Mike and Danielle could get a closer look.

Danielle read the acronym in the center circle of the page aloud: "**M.O.R.E.: MULTIPLE OPTIONS for RESULTS in EDUCATION.** In smaller writing, underneath those words, it read: "CREATING A BRAIN-FRIENDLY ENVIRONMENT TO ACCELERATE THE LEARNING PROCESS."

"What does that mean?" Danielle asked, referring to what she'd just read.

"We'll come back to your question in a little while, I promise. For now, take a look at the strategies for the classroom that all of our teachers are expected to acquire over time." Joyce pointed toward the smaller squares, rectangles, hexagons and diamonds that surrounded the circle and filled the page (see mind-map on page 48, and summary on page 223). Each one had one or more words inside of it that named a strategy, and each one was connected by a line to one of seven main ideas that were, in turn, each connected to the center circle.

"You see, when I first got here," Joyce explained, "the staff had created a very warm, loving environment for the kids. That is the foundation of IDS. All teachers were encouraged to be their own unique selves, just like the children were; and each had different approaches to teaching. This may have worked in the early days, but it was time for a new paradigm. The challenge was keeping alive the feelings of warmth while, at the same time, consistently providing learning strategies that would benefit all of the children."

"In order to have both a caring and competent faculty, it's important that everyone on board have two things." She lifted two fingers, one at a time. "A common language *and* a 'bag full of options' that is constantly expanding."

Joyce knew that these concepts were abstract, but could see that Mike and Danielle were leaning forward, open to hearing more, wanting to understand.

"Imagine being a surgeon in today's age of technology," she said. "What if you graduated from medical school 100 years ago, or even 15? Do you think it would be important to continue your studies?"

"Of course," Mike answered, "otherwise, how would you know the latest and best methods that are being invented and discovered to help your patients?"

"Exactly," Joyce replied. To be sure that Danielle understood her point, she looked at her and said, "Would you want to go to a surgeon who hadn't studied since he graduated from medical school?"

"No way, because he wouldn't know the best way to operate!" Danielle stated emphatically.

"That's right! You'd want your surgeon to be both caring and competent. Now, let's take that example into the classroom," Joyce said. "Then it makes sense that teachers should continue to study and train, to find the best ways to help students learn."

Mike and Danielle nodded in agreement.

Joyce continued her explanation of the "M.O.R.E.-map."

"One of the fastest growing fields in technology today is the study of the brain and how it learns. Neuroscientists are our modern-day explorers, constantly discovering new information about the brain, the body and how we function."

"All of the ideas in the *M.O.R.E. Approach* offer options for teachers to be able to teach children in ways that are 'BRAIN-FRIENDLY,' like it says here, so that learning can be both joyful and stimulating!" Joyce directed their attention back to the center of the map, ready to answer Danielle's earlier question.

"If I give you an example, Danielle, it might make this chart come alive more."

She continued, pointing to the words 'Brain-Breaks' in a yellow hexagon on the right side of the map. "Our teachers know that the brain needs a short rest after concentrated learning; so they'll give their students 'brain-breaks' periodically throughout a lesson. We use it for ourselves, as well, when we train together every week!"

"Here's another example," Joyce said, as she pointed to the term '12 Verbal Skills' in an orange rectangle on the lower right hand side of the map. "Our teachers took a course developed by *Performance Learning Systems*, where they learned 12 verbal skills, including 'positive phrasing.' At IDS, we share a common language. Everyone, including the parents, is familiar with the words 'positive phrasing.' We all know to state what we want to say so that it's uplifting and *focuses on what we want people to know or do*." Joyce beamed widely at everyone in the room.

"Every one of our teachers also attends basic *Kagan* training (see resources), where they learn the actual steps to make cooperative learning and brain-based learning come to life in the classroom. Everything we study is more than just theory. We see ourselves as practitioners, applying what works with our students, based on research."

"We also value having school administrators participate in our ongoing training programs. For instance, our Admissions Director regularly attends our faculty trainings in order to be aware of the latest programs at IDS, so that she can pass the newest information along to the parents of prospective students."

Joyce looked at Mike and Danielle and said, "Let's go back to the surgeon example. Would you want your surgeon to use one language, but his team to use a different language?"

"Of course not," Mike replied. "That would be dangerous."

"Exactly! By having our teachers and staff participating in training every week and throughout the year, we're all continually renewing ourselves and expanding our bag of options, as well as our language. We strive to be lifelong learners."

Mike wondered for a moment about whether or not he would fit into that category of "lifelong learner." After deciding the answer was "yes,"—based on his continuing education in college and his thirst for expanding his horizons—he reflected about what it would be like to be on the IDS faculty, especially how exciting and rich those Tuesday trainings might be. He admitted to himself that such training might be more rigorous and demanding than he'd be capable of handling comfortably; but he also realized that anything worth striving for is worth the extra effort and commitment required.

After pausing in order to give her listeners a chance to process what they were learning, Joyce said, "Training does two things. Besides keeping us at our best, it's also a time for all of us to bond. It's where the feeling of an 'IDS family' is established, especially as our school grows. Because the training is in workshop format, meaning that the participants get to interact with each other in a structured way, teachers who don't normally work together have an opportunity to connect. This strengthens our team. And for me, personally, it keeps me humble." She added with a grin, "After being here for seven years, they all know me too well."

Joyce laughed, "Some of the staff also know that I tease about being a 'workshop junkie,' and it's true. I am! My biggest fear is getting out of date. I've seen too many people in education who found themselves in that position."

Danielle wondered what it would be like if all teachers had the opportunity to train and study the way the teachers at IDS do. It seemed funny to her to think about her teachers going to school, though she could name a few who could really use it!

"It's one thing," Joyce declared, "to have a philosophy, a language and lots of strategies; but it's a whole other challenge to really live the philosophy." She pointed again to the center of the mind-map. "That's what this *M.O.R.E. Approach* is all about. It's a commitment to an Olympic mentality, where training means: 'the best keep getting better!' We can now ask, 'What *more* do we need to help our students be effective learners?'"

At that moment, Robert Marquez, the IDS facilities manager, walked over and greeted the group. He spoke to Joyce with enthusiasm, telling her that he and the facilities team had just completed new landscaping in the front of the school. He also wanted to show "Dr. Joyce" the great job they had done on lighting the new school sign. Robert knew that his news could wait until the next day, but he also knew how excited Joyce got whenever school initiatives were taken or improvements were made.

Joyce smiled, recognizing the pride Robert and his crew exemplified – the pride everyone at IDS takes in fitting all the pieces of the puzzle together – making the school special for both the students and the community.

She looked around at the group and asked, "How would you all feel about taking a walk to the front of the school so

I can see what Robert and his team have done? I'll just be a few minutes, and you all can meet me in the office. I think there are some homemade cookies in there."

It was perfect timing for a "brain-break!"

A+ Action Approach
Leadership Lessons

> **Develop a Lifelong Learning Mentality**
> Raising the bar can be exciting for some, but overwhelming for others.
> *A teacher relayed the story that, when she told her good friend that she wanted to teach at IDS, her friend replied, "Why would you want to work at a school where you're never good enough?"*
> *Later, the teacher thought to herself, "Hmm, how exciting to be at a school where there's always opportunity for growth and continuous improvement!"*
> Some people see the glass half full and some see the glass half empty. At IDS, we choose to see the glass half full!

Surviving Stormy Seas:
Learning to Deal with Resistance

The group enjoyed the colorful buildings and the greenery as they strolled down the wooden boardwalk toward the front of the school to meet up with Robert.

"Are you sure you have time to handle this sign right now, Joyce?" Pam asked.

"Absolutely," Joyce replied. Her seven years at IDS had taught her that being head of a school requires attention to people's needs. Turning to Mike and Danielle, Joyce said, "I've learned the importance of addressing situations that come up as quickly as possible."

When they reached the office, Joyce went off with Robert, while Marilyn, Mike, Danielle, Cornie and Pam got comfortable in the conference room, where they sat at a round table. The sliding glass doors overlooked a few classrooms and a playground, while the inner doors opened to the main office. And, indeed, a plateful of chocolate-chip cookies sat squarely in the center of the table. Marie Massara, the receptionist, welcomed the group and brought bottled water for everyone. They chatted idly and munched on cookies while waiting for Joyce to finish working with Robert.

Mike knew that to complete his project, he'd want more information about leadership and managing change. So, when Joyce stepped into the room and joined the group at the table, he initiated the conversation, "I know the school has changed a lot. Where does the psychology of change play in all of the things that have happened here?"

Joyce sat for a moment, pondering his question, then responded, "Being on the leading edge of change is not easy. First of all, it means keeping up with developments constantly. But that's the easy part." She turned and smiled at Cornie and Pam. "The challenging part, as some of us know all too well, is showing other people how to welcome and embrace the changes. Change causes different reactions in different people at different times. Talking about change is one thing, but implementing it is a different ballgame altogether! For some people, accepting a new idea can be frightening and even threatening."

"Why?" asked Danielle, as she looked at her light pink fingernails. She thought about how much she loved change and how she was always looking for new routes to ride her bike to school.

Joyce asked, "Remember when I spoke at the 35th Anniversary Celebration about Vasco da Gama's mission to find the route to the Indies by ship?"

"I remember that," replied Danielle. "You said that many people were afraid because they believed that the earth was flat. It was during the same time as Christopher Columbus." She smiled at Joyce, showing off her knowledge.

"What does that have to do with change *now*?" Danielle sounded confused.

"Well, today, we're *still* exploring; but now, the contemporary explorers are neuroscientists. They're exploring a new territory, gathering information about our *inner* world, through brain-research."

"But why should people be afraid of those kinds of explorations?" asked Danielle. "Especially if they make learning fun!"

Mike was eager to hear more.

"Let me explain this through a story," Joyce began. "Back in the winter of 1995, before coming to IDS, I took a 9-day self-help training program called Avatar, at the recommendation of my neighbor and good friend. Then, during my third year at IDS, in the spring of 1999, I got a flyer in the mail to take the follow-up course. This was at a time when I was trying to figure out better ways to help our teachers really reach the hearts of the children."

"After I had taken the follow-up course myself, I was convinced that this training would help the teachers immensely. Not only would they be able to reach the children better, it would also help them be more effective with parents and colleagues, as well as in their personal lives, in ways that would far exceed their current expectations. The strongest message of the training mirrored the IDS philosophy of teaching people to be more compassionate."

Joyce noticed that Mike was still holding Cornie's copy of the IDS philosophy and she asked him to read it. She pointed to the middle of the paragraph to get him started, and he read aloud, *"We consider it our responsibility to foster each child's capacity for learning, to help him/her grow morally, spiritually, and emotionally, as well as physically and intellectually. Recognizing the many differences in learning rates and styles, we believe in individualizing each child's school experience to whatever extent is possible for the fullest development of his/her potential. Our goal is to provide a relaxed, but stimulating atmosphere where each child feels acceptance and encouragement in the achievement of success through the exercise of responsible choice."*

Joyce looked up and said, "I got support from the Board to make the training available to the faculty, and from May to October of 1999, almost thirty staff members from IDS attended. People expressed excitement about getting tools to increase attention, focus and the ability to maintain a positive mental set. The course content aims to reduce prejudices, labels and judgments, while offering new tools to develop more meaningful connections. Actually, the tools are designed to make it easier to appreciate others and feel appreciated. It was my hope that the course would increase the chances for *every* child to feel valued and confident.

"Those who took the course represented a wide variety of backgrounds. Some were younger and some were older; they had varying years of teaching experience; and they came from four or five different religions. Yet everyone found some value in the course, and most found it to be the most incredibly powerful training they had ever experienced."

Mike stared at Joyce, and sensed, based on her change in tonality and body language, that something intense was about to happen in her story. Joyce looked at everybody and said, "Remember: often tucked behind enthusiasm lurks unexpected results."

Then her voice got a little louder and she wasn't smiling as she proceeded, "In November of the same year, the course became a major controversial issue here. A website was started by someone who was angry with the developer of the course, Harry Palmer, who was also the author of *Living Deliberately* and the founder of Star's Edge International. Someone at IDS found out about this man's website, and when he told me what he'd read, I dismissed it as unimportant because it sounded *so silly* and had nothing to do with what we experienced in the course. But when he told other people here at the school, rumors started to spread."

"This situation was a good example of living the challenges of leadership that many new programs or innovations first experience. Actually, it resembled the old gossip game, 'Telephone.' Some parents were afraid that their children were being taught material that was religious, which was obviously not true! This self-help course happened to be very effective and aligned with goals for teachers working to bring kids to their full potential. What I was beginning to discover was that perhaps we were ahead of our time."

"You see, some people panicked. As fear rose, reason went out to sea for even some of our highly educated parents; and instead of 'going to the source' to find out about the problem, parent concerns 'fueled the fire.'"

Mike and Danielle could tell that this story was not fun for Joyce to talk about.

"Even with all of my education and experience," she continued, "and the reputation I had earned as an educator, I could not stop rumors from growing out of hand. Judgments were made without knowledge, and accusations turned rumor and innuendo into a frenzy for some. Phone chaining, mistrust and rumor became the MO for a growing number of people. Personally, I was taken by surprise that people would doubt our intentions.

"At the same time, leadership requires that concerns are taken seriously." Joyce lowered her voice as she continued, "It was clear that we were in uncharted waters. We were having such terrific breakthroughs that would impact learners, but my limitations as a captain also became *very* evident."

After a moment spent wondering how much more to say to her small audience, she said, "Although the captain may know the destination, the question remains: Is the captain skilled enough to lead the crew there?"

Danielle interrupted, "But Joyce, I don't understand, why *would* people be so upset?" Then suddenly, a look of understanding came over Danielle's face, "Come to think of it, maybe I *do* understand. I know what rumors are like; they can really hurt a person. Someone spread rumors about a friend of mine being gay. Some of the boys would not hang out with him anymore, even his friends. I know him and none of it was true; but it really hurt his feelings! And even if it *were* true, people need to be respectful of people's differences."

"You're right, Danielle," Joyce continued. "Rumors can really hurt people. They can be very destructive. The problem happens when the listener accepts the rumor as factual. It gets out of hand when people spread it as truth without ever having gone to the source. Rumors often go unsubstantiated and then become hard to control."

"One day," she went on, "I received a letter from Bernie Haake, one of our former headmasters, and a member of the IDS Board of Trustees at the time. He had heard about the rumors, and from his long school leadership career, knew immediately that the waves were high and the boat was rocking. It describes so well what we were facing. I'll show you." Joyce went to get the letter from her office.

When she returned, she said, "This letter gives a good perspective on the challenges of leadership that go on behind the scenes." Then she handed the four-page, handwritten letter to Mike, who began reading aloud what Bernie had written:

"To enjoy a lengthy stay at one place, do nothing. Our schools are full of guys, mostly guys, who stay in the same place, or get a 'richer' job, because they have learned to do nothing while speaking the code words of 'quality,' 'improvement' and 'progress.'

So Joyce, go back to the future [to the university]. Vastly enriched by your stay in the "real world," you will now be infinitely better equipped to teach teachers how to teach in a world where all the strings are attached to people from yesterday...

Be satisfied. Go and share your skills and learnings fashioned from theory and reality with teachers and leaders of tomorrow who will be your multipliers.

I'm serious. Don't stay, don't burn out, quit while you're still ahead...
People like what they know (have experienced) and are fearful of the unknown. The more different, the more resistant to change...

...Did you know Pavlov's dogs were totally and completely disoriented when the cellar in which they were kept was flooded, and to save the dogs, their trainers had to submerge them momentarily underwater to get through a low doorway to safety outside? In that moment of stress, they "forgot" all their conditioning."

Mike stopped in the middle of reading the letter and exclaimed, "That's exactly what happens to people!"

Joyce responded, "Absolutely."

Mike then finished reading Bernie's letter aloud.

"Keep in mind how we as a nation are "behaving" in trying to change education, and compare that with how we as a nation behaved in response to Kennedy's challenge (mission) to get us to the moon before the Russians got there.

We did not try to remodel a 747! A clearly defined mission and timetable demanded new power sources, new strategies, new materials, new methods, new learnings, a totally new vehicle, new evaluation devices, new levels of expenditure and shedding of theories and experience which produced the 747... and I don't recall a vote on the matter and we did not turn the job over to Boeing!"

Mike stopped reading the letter, and Joyce smiled. She felt a deep appreciation for Bernie's insights, and said, "I loved the fact that he cared so much for me, to tell me to return to where I could be more successful; but in my heart, I knew that I needed to see this through. It would have been very easy to go back to where I felt appreciated." Then she laughed, adding, "Most of the time, anyway!"

"Sometimes, life decisions aren't easy," Mike thought to himself. "There's always something you have to give up." Aloud, he asked, "How did you make your decision, Joyce?"

"Coincidentally," she said, "at the same time that all of this was occurring, my leave of absence from the university, which had been extended for four years, was being called in for me to make a decision. So now I was faced with a dilemma. Do I stay at IDS or return to the university? Where did I really want to commit my time to make learning more humane and model a 'brain-friendly' environment?"

Joyce took out a typewritten letter and said, "In a letter to the Dean of the College of Education at the time, I explained my decision to continue my stay here, rather than return to the university." She began to read from the letter:

"... As you know, I am currently completing my fourth year on leave of absence from USF to lead Tampa's Independent Day School. I originally took this position because I felt a strong need 1) to "WALK THE TALK," 2) to transfer theory into practice, and 3) to gain a sense of the day-to-day challenges of leadership, learning and life at a school site.

...Thanks to the college's generosity in granting my leave, I have succeeded in the above goals. I have also discovered that the many authors who attempt to develop models for change in an organization are clearly on target and often prophetic. I naively believed that the change process in schools could evolve quickly and overcome unexpected resistances as long as the right motives and strategies were in place ... NOT!

...I remember reading books that inspired me to teach in the Chicago inner city, written by people who were determined to change the world. I remember thinking, 'Why did people quit so soon (after one year)?' In fact, it's easier

to write books about the 'insider's view' of a school or system involved in change than it is to see it through the resistances that emerge. Innovations abruptly interrupted often leave behind people who were initially inspired to move forward, who are left with the disappointment, debacle, and dilemma about what to do next. I have asked myself: 'Is this hypocrisy? Is this ethical? Or is this just the way things are done?'

It seems to take five to seven years for innovations to take hold, begin to establish some credence, and evolve naturally within the system. For me to fully leave IDS now to return to USF would feel totally unethical, unaligned, and even irresponsible. I often wish the "resistors" to change would have succeeded so I could write a best seller. I even have the title: 'Will Education Ever Change: NOT'. The Board at IDS, to their credit, wants to move forward, and I am compelled by their sincerity and their devotion to children and the future to accept their request to extend my position at the school. I have no other choice, if I am to face my conscience daily with any sense of integrity.

...Somewhere, we as educators need to show what can be accomplished when change is sustained through its evolutionary phases . . . Somewhere we have to heal the wounds and support those who dare to step out front, willing to take on the resistances, challenges, and joy that emanate from persistence, community, and teamwork. Somewhere we have to demonstrate the bridge between what and how we train at the university, and how it is practiced in the schools.

...Student success will be what drives the future!

...That is what compels me to continue with my passion to facilitate a school environment where we can truly bridge the gap between 'knowledge' and 'practice.'"

The group was silent for a few moments, each person taking in the message in his or her own way.

Mike ended the pause as he said with deep respect, "Sounds like you went through quite a storm, Joyce. I'll bet there were a lot of A+ Action Approach learned."

"Hm-m-m…" Joyce reflected upon his comment, and said, "Actually the experience ended up being a good one because it helped clarify my personal and professional goals."

And then she went on in her familiar style; Joyce raised one finger at a time as she reviewed her lessons out loud, "First, I learned, hands-on, that being the change-agent often means becoming the target of resistance. What would I have done differently?" she asked, as she raised a second finger. "Bring in the experts… So many professionals, nationally, who had taken the course, could have been called upon to validate the strength and powerful potential of it. This might have brought reason and appreciation to what we were trying to accomplish, and truth could have defeated rumor. Sometimes leaders become blind-sided by their own naïve invincibility, and that's what happened to me. I tried to handle too much of it on my own."

"Every new idea in history," Joyce said, as her third finger joined the other two, "created resistance until people had time to live with it and see the results. Leading means being responsible for making changes. Expect resistance. The key is having the perseverance to work through it."

"Most of all," Joyce lowered her voice for emphasis, as she raised her fourth finger, "I learned that meeting change requires commitment to following one's heart. Before, this was a theory that I talked about. Now I knew, first hand, and had the opportunity to meet the storm head on and stay the course, sailing toward the sunshine! And I'm glad I did." Anne Frank's words, which were often a comfort to her, rang through Joyce's mind. She shared, "I believe in the sun, even when it rains."

A+ Action Approach
Leadership Lessons

➤ **Proceed Purposefully**
When introducing innovation, be careful about pockets of information that are susceptible to being filled with damaging rumors; rumors can destroy the very innovation that could empower people's lives.

➤ **Persevere and Persist**
- Being the change-agent means being the target of resistance.
- Bring in the experts to strengthen the credibility for making change.
- Every significant new idea creates resistance until people have time to live with it and see the results.
- Leading means making changes.
- Expect resistance.
- Meeting change requires commitment to following one's heart.

The Tide Turns With A Charted Course

"What did you do to bring things back to normal, Joyce?" asked Mike.

"Everything new that I brought to this school has met some level of resistance. Passing through those stages with dignity and respect is important. So, in this case, we created new avenues of communication. Although communication lines were always there – we always had an open door policy, easy access to teachers, a Board that would be responsive to calls, and opportunities for people to learn more through newsletters and press releases – still, this was a time to add more structure."

"'Building a true learning community' took on new meaning. When a good system is set in place, people can use that as a forum to create change, rather than engage in finger-pointing; so we created strategies that brought order and understanding to make our team stronger."

Joyce reflected for a moment and continued, "We created new forums for communication, like expanding 'Coffee Talks' and adding 'Edu-Talks,' where we answered questions and helped people get clear about what was happening. We kept stepping forward, even though it was hard to do sometimes. We sent out press releases emphasizing the positive experiences at IDS, and we put the focus back where it belonged..."

"On the kids!" exclaimed Mike and Danielle together.

Marilyn, Cornie, Pam and Joyce laughed.

Joyce smiled, "Right on! Now this took time, patience and perseverance on the part of many people. The Board was relieved when I decided that, because of the controversy, it would be best to withdraw the Avatar course from the professional menu for the IDS faculty, even though other states would soon begin to recognize its value for education. From that point onward, all teacher training at IDS would be research-based and/or what was considered 'best practices' in educational circles. The most important thing was to keep the focus on the students."

Mike noted silently that, once again, the timeless philosophy of IDS stood strong. Even during the rockiest of storms, Joyce and the IDS leaders would focus on what was best for the children. Images arose in his mind, of the American flag still standing after the Revolutionary War and after "9-11." He shared his reflections out loud with the group.

Joyce replied, "Mike, that's a beautiful vision, thank you." It was time to bring the session to an end. "I hope you learned a lot today and have some good information for your paper. Do you have any questions?"

Mike turned to Joyce and said, "I certainly do, thank you. The main one is, could you help me summarize the A+ Action Approach, something I could use as an outline for my paper?"

"Sure, I'd be happy to," Joyce replied as she walked up to the large whiteboard that took up the space on one of the walls.

She picked up a purple dry-erase marker and across the top of the board wrote:

**"An A+ Action Approach to Leadership:
7 Components of Effective Leadership and Change"**

In the middle of the board, in green, she drew two circles with eight short spokes stemming from the outer circle. In between the two circles, she wrote:

"Change Process"

It looked like a ship captain's wheel. The top spoke pointed to the title.

Next to each spoke, Joyce wrote:

ACTION: Model the Models
ACTION: Embrace a Vision
ACTION: Proceed Purposefully: Do Whatever It Takes
ACTION: Build Leadership Capacity, Teams & Networks
ACTION: Adopt "Presence"
ACTION: Develop a Lifelong Learning Mentality
ACTION: Persevere and Persist

As soon as she concluded her summary, Mike stepped up to the board and along the bottom of the board, he wrote:

"DO WHAT'S BEST FOR THE KIDS!"

Mike turned to face his expectant audience and shared that, in his college paper he would cite many examples from the history of IDS to demonstrate his new understandings of leadership and change, using the insights that he'd gained from his interviews.

Then he said, "Thanks, everyone, for all of your help on my research project. And thanks for creating a school where kids can really be happy." He looked over at Marilyn and said, "Thanks, Grandma, for making today happen; this was great. You've always known, Grandma, that it's all about kids!"

"And so, while my leadership development professor will be the only person to read this as a research paper, all the rest of you will read it as what it really is... the story of Independent Day School: Corbett Campus."

Danielle smiled brightly and innocently brought a close to the session by saying, "Thank you, Joyce, Cornie and Pam, the teachers at IDS, and everyone who cared to keep our grandmothers' dreams alive and for making IDS such a great place for kids. I hope that I'll have teachers who feel that way about education. I wish all my teachers could come to the Tuesday trainings at IDS."

"Well, maybe... anything is possible!" Joyce said with a knowing smile.

* * * * * * * * * * * * * * * * * *

Mike, Danielle and Johnny are fictional characters created for the purpose of sharing the IDS story with you, the reader.

The rest of the names and events reflect the historical evolution of Independent Day School in Tampa, Florida, based on interviews with many people, including the original founders, current school administrators and Board of Trustees, as well as teachers and parents who have been with IDS since its beginnings.

Thanks to all who contributed their time.

It's All About Kids!

PART II
Living the Philosophy
by Dr. Joyce Burick Swarzman

"Our mission statement, from 1968, created by our founders Marilyn Gatlin and Betty Anderson, has always presented a challenge about how to enact and combine a nurturing atmosphere with demanding academics, a relaxed, yet stimulating environment and cooperation within today's competitive world. To achieve these apparent contradictions, we are exploring and will continue to explore all the best approaches to reach our children, including workshops, training, and giving teachers the tools and skills to continually improve in their profession. IDS is committed to promoting best practices in education. Best practices include research-based strategies about learning and/or programs recognized by educational businesses or associations."

–*Excerpt from a letter to parents, May 15, 2000*
Written by Cornelia Corbett
President, Board of Trustees,
1981-1985, 1992-2002

A Three-Pronged Approach

Today's field of education is blessed with eloquent philosophies, mission statements and/or powerful ideas, ideals, goals and objectives.

Processes developed to engage teams, groups and organizations are prevalent, systematic and often inspiring. Capturing a vision and motivating people to rally behind it certainly takes skill and commitment to a higher purpose.

That is all well and good, but the ongoing challenge is just how to combine the philosophy and mission statement with the practical day-to-day aspects of education.

In our case, the 35-year old IDS philosophy is as relevant today as it was when our two founders, Marilyn Gatlin and Betty Anderson, launched their dream and established Independent Day School in 1968. The bottom line of this timeless philosophy is "children first."

A three-pronged approach has been used to translate the rhetoric into reality:

1 RESOURCES:

Provide teachers with an abundance of resources to support all aspects of teaching and learning in their classrooms and throughout the campus to get the best results for students.

Result:

Teachers here have grown to expect the resources necessary to support all aspects of teaching and learning. All available resources are dedicated to supporting the classrooms and the classroom environment.

2   FACULTY DEVELOPMENT:

Identify and develop a faculty known for their life-long learning focus, and instill the Olympic Mentality Model into all we do as educators; whereby the best are always working to be better. In the Olympics, it's called "Going for the Gold" or breaking and creating new records. For our own purposes, "winning" means both teachers and students win when we strive for excellence in the classroom. Look up to the sky – there's plenty of room at the top!

Result:

Teacher training and study are part of what we do here at IDS. We believe that:

> - It is an expectation.
> - It is a recruiting tool for new faculty.
> - It is what brings other educators to learn from and with us.
> - It is what gives the teachers confidence and a sense of enthusiasm to provide learning that is productive, applicable, and speaks to the self-worth of each child.
> - It means building in THE TIME for study, reflection, and *review, review, review.* With afternoon in-services, half-day releases, in-service days and a week of intensive training prior to school opening each year, we provide the clear message that *we are a culture that supports a life-long learning mentality.*

3   LEARNING STRATEGIES:

Transform the educational process and accelerate learning through strategies that:

> - Allow all students to achieve and soar with

greater ease and more satisfaction.

> Generate more alignment with the natural development of children at all ages and stages.

Just as the computer improved the speed of communication, the car improved the efficiency and enjoyment of travel, and the electric stove increased the speed and creativity of cooking, so too should we be on a journey to accomplish contemporary and innovative advancements in learning. Thus, we are on a mission to create a brain-friendly environment.

Result:

The creation of the *M.O.R.E. Approach* for staff development: Multiple Options for Results in Education. The IDS *M.O.R.E. Approach* identifies seven components and over one hundred strategies that act as a foundation for creating a dynamic, high achieving learning community.

The *M.O.R.E.* Approach
(Multiple Options for Results in Education)
is All About Staff Development

Attention to training is critical when building the capacity of our greatest human resource in a school setting: the TEACHER! Developing Teachers, with a capital "T." It might sound corny, but anyone running a school soon learns that it is essential. Education is all about kids and the teachers they encounter. **Teachers make the difference!**

The IDS position on teacher training is driven by three basic directives:
1) Research-based learning strategies
2) Programs recognized by national education associations or respected educational companies
3) General strategies identified as "Best Practices" in education

All areas chosen are designed to accomplish three purposes:
1) Accelerate the learning process
2) Increase time on, and attention to, classroom tasks, which correlate to increased academic achievement
3) Provide teachers with an abundance of options to connect positively and effectively with the academic, emotional, social and physical needs of learners

Perhaps what makes IDS unique in its approach is that:
1) We seek to implement best practices **ALL AT ONCE**; and,
2) We seek to create an entire school of excellence, rather than settle for pockets of excellence.

If parents and visitors come to observe cooperative learning, they also witness the implementation of a number of other skills or strategies being utilized in combination with a cooperative structure. A multiple implementation strategy requires a highly skilled teacher, able and willing to continuously refine, review, and redirect efforts to meet both class and individual needs. Sounds great, right? Right! The truth is, we are only as good as the tools we have available to us today. What was modeled for most of us during our time as students is in dire need of revision.

Most of us have experienced school as: a) sitting in rows for long periods of time, b) learning primarily through lectures, print and memorization, and c) an over-reliance on drilling information without always experiencing understanding.

IDS has transcended that limited model of learning by developing the *M.O.R.E. Approach*, designed to reach the uniqueness in all learners.

The *M.O.R.E. Approach* includes basic generic skills in teacher facilitation, or trainer effectiveness, from a variety of diverse sources.

Each *M.O.R.E. Approach* strategy helps accelerate the learning process by always keeping in mind the importance of a brain-friendly environment for learners.

The *M.O.R.E. Approach* is divided into 7 major components (as shown on the map):

- **Child-Centered Vision**
- **Appreciating The Uniqueness Of The Learner**
- **Motivational Strategies To Increase Time On Task**
- **Creating Dignity And Respect**
- **Teacher/Student Presence: Making Connections**
- **Learning Community**
- **Curriculum Development**

Skills and strategies comprise each major component and are easily attainable through study and practice. In reality, this teaching technology is not truly innovative, but what has already been identified as "best practice" in education.

The *M.O.R.E. Approach* focuses only on strategies or programs that apply to ALL learners in ALL grade levels and ALL subject areas. In addition to studying the components within the *M.O.R.E. Approach*, our teachers also stay on the cutting edge in their specific subject areas by attending workshops and conferences which address curriculum strategies that enhance subject areas, such as Math, Language Arts, Science, Social Studies, Spanish, Art, Music, P.E. and Technology.

More On the *M.O.R.E. Approach*

People are in search of answers. Common concerns from both home and school often produce statements such as: "You need to pay more attention to your work!", "Where is your willpower to succeed?", "Why do you let others influence you?", "Why aren't kids kinder to each other?", "Why can't you think for yourself?", and "You need more confidence – Believe in yourself – You can do it!" Books are written on these topics, educational conferences are held based on these themes, parents are searching for answers, and teachers work tirelessly to manage classrooms and address these common concerns.

The *M.O.R.E. Approach* offers a solution to these familiar questions through a synergistic methodology in which the whole is greater than the sum of its parts. Each component weaves into the concepts of the next, opening up possibilities for reaching the "whole child."

The *M.O.R.E. Approach* includes a variety of sources that reflect the diversity of learners and their learning processes. For example, in the book *Quantum Teaching*, by Bobbie DePorter, Mark Reardon and Sarah Singer-Nourie, the authors conclude that to "orchestrate student success," teachers need to be highly skilled in how to: build the power of positive interactions, build rapport, tap into the joy of learning, develop the warmth of belonging, and create an environment that is full of excitement, intrigue and success.

Other authors we study recognize that a person's own comfort zone and beliefs, whether conscious or unconscious, can limit or unleash one's potential. For example, by studying the *M.O.R.E.* sections on Curriculum, Learning Community, and Motivational Strategies, IDS students are then able to experience the wisdom of these teachings as implemented by their teachers.

This "teacher wisdom" emanates from continuously exploring ways to:

1) Increase attention skills deliberately, and decrease scattered or fixed attention
2) Build the capacity to have personal ownership of one's will, or willpower
3) Develop a greater connection and rapport with others
4) Turn the "I can't" beliefs that limit one's potential into "I CAN"
5) Help educators truly apply recommendations from "how to" books like *Quantum Teaching.*

There is an overwhelming abundance of information that is eloquently making available more and more updated knowledge about the learning process and the brain-mind-body connection.

The *M.O.R.E. Approach* has embraced many of those sources. However, in order for change to reach all classrooms, it will take a lot of collaboration by educational designers and researchers, so that all of us who are practitioners can more readily progress beyond traditional methods that truly serve only a portion of the population. That is why we seek to attract teachers who:

1) Can balance what we do know today with an imagination of future possibilities
2) Can engage in meaningful conversations about teaching and learning
3) Have the willingness to move forward and implement "best practices" that will continuously provide more challenging, relevant and interesting work and opportunities for students
4) Can problem-solve collaboratively and positively as part of a team, believing that *"all of us are smarter than one of us"*

5) Are passionate about children, the joy of learning, and the future.

Obviously, accomplishing this task takes energy, commitment, and leaders who embrace an A+ Action Approach to Leadership and Change, or something like it. It is far easier to blame the system, parents, teachers or society than it is to change. The *M.O.R.E. Approach*, with its attention to deliberately seeking "OPTIONS, OPTIONS, and more OPTIONS," is an attempt to go beyond dialogue and JUST DO IT! The aim is to serve our student population well, along with the greater community.

Lesson Planning and Life's Lessons Have a Lot in Common

Examining life's paradoxes reveals lessons for the classroom on how to "Bring the Philosophy to Life"

Today's Expectations:

Did you ever consider that yesterday's innovations have become today's expectations, while today's expectations will be replaced by tomorrow's innovations? So where does that leave education today?

The traditional model of education: students seated in rows of chairs repeat the pattern of "read the chapter, answer the questions, take the test," mirrors the industrial model from the early 1900's, when information was contained and predictable. In order to keep pace with today's information age, this model is being replaced by major 21st century breakthroughs in understanding how the human brain is wired.

Through imaging techniques, neuroscientists are able to gain remarkable information about what occurs inside the human brain. PET Scans, CAT Scans and MRI's reveal how different information, experiences and chemicals created by the body affect the brain and how it functions. The *M.O.R.E. Approach* selects materials and techniques designed to embrace brain-friendly strategies by focusing not only on what children learn, but also on *how* they learn.

Paradox: Life's Search for Balance

In a "Power Talk" audio tape, Anthony Robbins identifies six basic human needs. These needs parallel the work of educators like Eric Jenson, who translated brain research into "education-ese."

Understanding what Robbins calls the "Six Basic Human Needs" assists teachers in creating a balance between the "paradoxes of needs" that the brain craves. The six basic needs serve as a helpful model in posing questions about how to successfully engage students in meaningful ways to achieve that brain-friendly environment.

According to Robbins, the six basic human needs, described below, fall into three categories, creating an overall framework for applying different learning strategies. When delivering lessons, finding the correct balance between 1) certainty and uncertainty, 2) significance and connectedness, and 3) growth and contribution helps teachers tap into the uniqueness of each individual.

Utilizing this model of paradoxes in lesson planning keeps the focus on the child, rather than on the innovation; at IDS, we use the following education-friendly terminology to communicate the above ideas:

TRADITION & NOVELTY:

All people require some level of certainty in their lives. In school, that translates into implementing strategies that provide routines, schedules, a guarantee of physical and emotional safety, consistency of deeds, a sense of stability and an appreciation for specific traditions. However, too much routine may result in complacency and a "ho-hum" attitude.

Novelty, or a sense of uncertainty, plays a role in injecting excitement, energy and enthusiasm into the curriculum. It translates into lessons that provide variety, surprise and even the unexpected. Trips, projects and intriguing lessons offer the hooks to attract the students' interest and engage them meaningfully. Finding a balance between routine and novelty requires a deliberate analysis of each lesson or series of lessons. The task is further complicated by each person's definition of novelty. Too much for one is too little for another. This often requires a magician in the role of teacher.

INDIVIDUALISM & RELATIONSHIPS:

Every human being wants to feel significant and valued. Attaining a sense of self-worth brings joy within each of us. In the classroom, students consciously or unconsciously want to be appreciated for who they are. Everyone raising more than one child or having grown up with siblings can remember from experience that each child responded to different forms of praise and received joy from succeeding in different venues.

Some individuals thrive on public recognition, while others prefer quiet acknowledgment. Each individual needs some dose of "ego recognition." Without a sense of significance, children may seek attention through unacceptable behaviors or even withdraw into a passive "I could care less" mode.

On the other hand, too much self-importance can lead to an absence of social skills needed to function as healthy adults. Connectedness relates to cooperation and respect for others, including their space, ideas and differences. It helps build relationships that promote caring and a sense of belonging within the classroom. It affirms the belief that "all of us are smarter than one of us." Connectedness also refers to linking the curriculum with experiences that are meaningful and have real-life application. Spencer Kagan's "Cooperative Learning" strategies are some of the many ways that we seek to bridge content and connectedness. This proven strategy assists teachers in fostering a team environment, which encourages everyone to work for the good of the whole and yet allows for individual recognition.

PERSONAL GROWTH AND SERVICE TO THE GREATER GOOD:

Growth involves the ability to spread our wings into areas that renew and allow us to build upon our natural abilities. For an adult, this may include personal growth seminars or professional experiences that stretch us to think or act differently. For students, it may include participating in band, chorus, a play, joining a sports team or taking a special course that advances the student's own personal interests. Taking part in these types of activities fosters a life-long learning mentality and often leads to personal discovery, motivation and even exhilaration.

Service refers to contribution beyond self-interest. Having an impact on others without asking anything in return lifts the human spirit. In lesson planning, service to the greater community should be an important part of student learning. Service builds an appreciation for our own families, as well as the greater community. Volunteerism models the joy of giving just by the act of doing.

<u>**SUMMARY**</u>:

Application of "brain-friendly" findings clearly takes teaching methods and lesson planning from the realm of innovation to a level of daily expectation.

The articles and stories in Parts III and IV capture a glimpse into how IDS provides this wealth of brain-compatible experiences for our students to balance the opposing ideas of: tradition and novelty, individualism and relationships, personal growth and service to the greater good.

Innovation Requires Change

Change conjures up a multitude of reactions and almost always meets with resistance. Underlying resistance, actually, is fear about the unknown and fear for the potential loss of certainty and safety. Everything new at IDS has met some level of resistance from teachers, parents, and students, at times. Joel Barker, the futurist, in his video, *Paradigm Pioneers*, reminds the viewer that if you wait for everyone to go forward, you'll continue to wait.

It seems that reactions to innovation include: 20% of the people eager and willing to go forward, 20% interested, 20% thinking, "I'll wait to see what happens," 20% verbally second-guessing the results, and 20% thinking, "Over my dead body."

For a moment, imagine living during the last turn of the century (1890-1910), when the horse and buggy was replaced by faster, more efficient transportation, and when movement from an agricultural society to an industrial society was rapidly picking up pace. Can you imagine the resistance to the automobile from those people who cherished those horse-drawn wagons and buggies?

Can you also imagine what it must have been like to move from farms and sprawling land to cities? Suddenly, the influx of children of these new factory-working, city-dwellers needed to be served. Schooling "as they knew it" changed from a 1 to 2-room school concept, with Multi-Age classrooms where everyone learned together and from each other, to an educational process that geared up to educate and regiment the masses. Changes included: 1) school construction modeled after factories, 2) adoption of a grade-by-age classroom, based on the mid-19th century German model of schooling, 3) classrooms designed for children to sit in rows, where silence was honored and obedience was demanded, and 4) dispensing information went from teacher to student, where working alone was now expected (similar to a factory worker where the focus was on his/her part of the assembly line, without much attention to the other pieces or the end result).

All around us, change is occurring at a rapid pace... yet "schooling" is still designed based on the industrial model, looking more like a "horse and buggy" everyday.

We understand so much more about learning today. The rapid scientific discoveries about how the brain learns, accesses, processes and spits out information are only trickling down to education. Books and workshops are in abundance with knowledgeable people crying out for the need to change the learning environment to make it more brain compatible.

But human nature, often our greatest ally, in this case, may be our greatest challenge because change causes different levels of resistance in different people at different times. The study of the change process provides many insights about how resistance is played out in the midst of innovation. It is common to expect people to experience one or more of the following types of resistance when faced with change: annoyance with those excited about the possibilities; feeling awkward and self-conscious when having to do something new; worrying about what might be lost or has to be given up; feeling overwhelmed, as though there is too much to do or handle; sensing that some are more ready than others to move forward; using a lack of resources as an excuse to retreat or slow up the process; and/or reverting back to old behavior when the pressure is off to move forward.

Understanding the nature of resistance to change paves the way for how to proceed with new ideas or innovations. The key is to keep the best of what the "horse and buggy" in education has to offer, while welcoming the introduction of innovation. To accomplish this, it is often necessary to take a "big step," because "you can't cross a chasm in two small jumps."[1] That's how we have approached our faculty: keep what works, but add where we can do better!

Dissonance is a natural outcome of change. The real test of success is a *willingness* to meet each resistance with an opportunity to find a solution that makes the outcome even better. Creating a culture that accepts, protects, nurtures and supports change efforts is critical for leadership that is charged with moving an institution or organization forward.

---

[1] *Quote by David Lloyd George, Former Prime Minister of Britain, 1863-1945.*

Note: Special thanks to Dr. Robert Anderson, leading national educator, for his guidance in securing historical data in this chapter.

Harvard Professor Rosabeth Moss Kanter, author of *Change Masters*, gives comforting advice about the change process: the vision of what is to come excites everyone and the final results give great pride; but in the middle, everything looks, feels and often sounds like the disaster of witnessing a house being built.

Exploring options and venturing outside the boundaries of standard convention has led to the discovery of a round earth versus one that is flat, trips to the moon, cars, faxes, computers and a belief that all students can be winners everyday!

PART III

Edu-Talk: Teacher Stories
Creating an Extraordinary Context for Learning

Is student success more about class size or is it more about teacher effectiveness? If we had to choose, teacher effectiveness would be the first priority. Highly qualified teachers are as important as highly qualified surgeons. Surgeons operate on bodies, while teachers operate on the minds and psyches of the learning capabilities of each student.

When teachers at IDS shared their views of teaching, found in the following section, it was rare for them to mention the curriculum, the particular subject matter that they teach, or even their favorite lesson. More often, they offered stories about creating meaningful connections with their students, helping their students work together, and creating a context for learning that is safe, effective, and fun. This may sound misleading, as though the teachers need to emphasize academics more. The opposite is true, however.

Students with various abilities at IDS excel academically, and many are a year or more ahead of state benchmarks, achieving high average Stanine scores on national tests. This is a result of a rigorous curriculum combined with a positive, even magical atmosphere. In addition to elevated levels of learning, students enjoy participating in extracurricular activities, displaying a healthy balance between personal and academic growth.

At IDS, it is all happening at once, in one place. Each one of the following stories contains one or more components of the *M.O.R.E. Approach*. Each story alone is significant and part of a very good school. The strength here is the abundance of brain-friendly experiences that occur continuously throughout the school.

The stories in Part III range from people's joy of working in a dynamic learning community to reflections about handling bullies. Where many books on education emphasize academics and curriculum, we have chosen to focus on aspects of education that can benefit teachers with situations they face every day, such as motivation, behavior and time on-task. With these issues successfully met, academic learning can take place with greater ease.

Each teacher's story or thought captures the essence of Teachers with a capital "T," working hard to make powerful connections with learners – not just connections for the sake of connections, but for the ultimate in achievement. That means achievement academically, socially and emotionally.

The "teacher" stories in this section are divided into four categories:

1. **Balancing Novelty and Routine in Lesson Planning**
2. **Group Dynamics – Making Connections:** *Personal and Professional Growth for Kids*
3. **Behavioral Lessons:** *Social, Emotional and Academic*
4. **Empowerment for Teachers, Parents and the Community:** *Personal and Professional Joy and Satisfaction*

Balancing Novelty and Routine in Lesson Planning

Ships Ahoy!

Jessica Schew, Pre-Kindergarten Teacher
At IDS since 1999

When it came time for planning our yearly "Welcome to IDS" unit, our Early Primary team realized that we were in the mood for something new! The idea was to create a unit embracing the values and responsibilities of our daily lives here in Pre-K and kindergarten, while greeting our newest additions with a memory to last a lifetime. The answer was "Ships Ahoy!"

On the first day of school, each Pre-K and kindergarten teacher dressed up in a white and blue sailing uniform and captain's hat. We greeted our sailors with "welcome aboard," introducing ourselves as the captains of the ship (our classroom). We explained that we were about to set sail on an incredible adventure, an adventure that would teach us everything we needed to be sure we would have a terrific year!

The teachers led a scavenger hunt to familiarize these young IDSers with their new school campus. They were to find the necessary items to set sail, including a rope, a compass and an anchor. The final stop on our hunt gave us the most important piece to our Ships Ahoy unit, our map. On the map, we learned about six different-colored destinations, each of which would teach the students an important lesson during subsequent days.

Here is a brief description of our itinerary. Our destination for day one was an adventure that took us to the Red River, where we came upon a red monster. This red monster shared about the importance of values, by making us realize that we needed values for our classroom so that our "ship" could always be a safe and happy place.

Day two's destination brought us to a new color with new values to incorporate into our learning community. The color was blue, and we learned about safety as we read the book *Blueberries for Sal* by Robert McCloskey. We discussed being safe on our campus by always having a buddy when walking from one building to another.

On destination day three, which was orange, we learned about privileges and responsibility. We visited the playground and talked about how it was a privilege to have such a great playground, and that it was our responsibility to use it the safest way.

During our fourth day's destination, purple, we learned about choices while we read the book *Harold and the Purple Crayon* by Crockett Johnson.

The message of destination day five: Try it! You might like it! We read *Green Eggs and Ham* by Dr. Seuss and made green eggs and ham, then talked about being open-minded about our snack-time food choices.

We learned, on destination day six, that many heads are better than one. A teamwork book we enjoyed was *The Crayon Box That Talked,* by Shane Derolf and Michael Letzig, which emphasizes the importance of appreciating diversity by asking, "Which would you enjoy more, a book that was all blue or purple, or a book that was bursting with lots of colors?" In our class, we are a variety of "beautiful crayons." Alone, we make a nice looking picture. Together we make an extraordinary masterpiece! We also make a point to recognize each child for being an "expert" in something. By tapping into each person's strengths and differences, we learn to understand and appreciate each other.

Every year, our Early Primary team works together to create a new theme that teaches and reinforces the timeless concepts mentioned above. We divide the jobs according to our strengths and passions. For example, this year, one team member gathered books, another person made costumes, and a third teacher created passports or color-coded maps. We always make three of everything, one for each of our classes. This type of teamwork takes extra time on our part, but it is worth every effort.

By creating lessons that allow our children to explore classroom values, they begin to integrate the concepts. Soon, ownership of these basic life values becomes the culture and is accepted as our way of life.

"Eye Can"

Jean Harrison, Kindergarten Teacher
At IDS since 1998

This year I made an 'Eye Can' can. It's a see-through can with little plastic eyeballs in it. If a student says the words, "I can't," then he or she gets the 'EYE CAN' and shakes it, repeating "I CAN! I CAN! I CAN! I CAN!"

I had to use that approach only once this year. That has been one of my biggest successes, to know that their prior negative thoughts more easily turned into an awareness of positive words, even for kindergarteners. My students learn to look for options and/or say, "I need some help." Those are the words that lead to solutions and option-seeking choices. Now, these kids feel like they *can* do anything. That's what matters to me!

If they work to maintain that "I Can" mentality their whole lives, then I know they've been given a great beginning.

Team Teaching Makes It Real!

Roberta Lipschutz, Kindergarten Teacher
At IDS since 1986

It was President's weekend and my teammate and I created a "historical conversation" to help our kindergarten classes compare and contrast George Washington and Abraham Lincoln. All of the teachers dressed for the part.

I wore a paper wig I created, complete with rolled white paper curls, and a white ruffled shirt. Cindy (my teammate) had a stovepipe hat, a black coat, and a construction paper beard. Dressed as the presidents, we had a conversation comparing our lives. "I lived on a big plantation and had my own horse," I said, gesturing to the photograph of the plantation on the easel. "Well, I lived in a small log cabin with my family and we were very poor," said "Abe." We compared our lives in such a way that the children could visualize the two men communicating as "real people," rather than one-dimensional historical characters from a book.

One of our follow-up activities, to assess the information they learned, was the Kagan cooperative structure, *Show Me*. Each child was given a blue card with the word "yes" and a red card with the word "no." A variety of questions were then posed to the class. For example, "George Washington learned to write using coal on the back of a shovel..."

I would say, "Think, think, think." The students remained quiet for 3 to 5 seconds, allowing for pause time, and then I said, "Show me!" When I said "Show me," they quickly raised the card of their choice. At a glance, we could determine, by the color of the raised cards, who understood and retained the information and who needed to receive additional instruction.

Presenting a lesson in this manner allowed our children to get a "real life" sense of historically significant political leaders and to demonstrate individual accountability through an instant assessment procedure. It was thrilling for us to see that every child was able to answer all the questions correctly. This was a powerful and fun lesson for us, too!

Source: Kagan Cooperative Learning

The KOW Kid

Debi Brockmeyer, First Grade Teacher
Primary Co-Division Leader
At IDS since 1981

Each child is unique and every child has the right to be celebrated. It just feels good. Feeling good works. Our children look forward to coming to school to learn! Appreciating others for their uniqueness also creates a safe and supportive climate conducive to learning academic skills.

Our class has a program called KOW, "Kid of the Week," where each child is celebrated and in turn learns to celebrate and appreciate others.

Each child is assigned one week out of the school year which is devoted to learning about and appreciating him or her, with all of his or her special qualities. We meet the family (including the family pet!), enjoy childhood stories through a timeline, learn about jobs, view pictures and gain a respect for that student's characteristics.

Making the "KOW Kid" a special book of compliments and appreciation concludes the week. The students in the class lovingly make each page. Every KOW Kid comes away from the experience feeling unique, cared for and very special. Tolerance and respect for others are an added bonus!

Brain-Breaks in the Classroom: Fire Up Those Neurons!

Jen Jones, Primary Multiage Teacher, Grades 1&2
At IDS since 1999

I love the results of integrating 'brain-breaks' throughout my teaching day; they get the students up and moving, and the change of pace does them wonders!

There are many different kinds of activities we can use for brain-breaks. Some are quietly done in seated positions, while others require movement and sound. Some take just 30 seconds, while others take two to five minutes.

I can see when the students are starting to become restless and even drained; it's written all over their faces. So, it's just amazing to watch a single, short activity reinvigorate a whole classroom full of students, allowing them to re-focus on what they need to do.

For instance, yesterday we were doing observational trials, where each group had to repeatedly time one aspect of a science experiment, with each trial lasting three minutes. The groups had different things to time; however, the activity eventually began to lose its energy, due to the repetition of these trials over and over again.

So, we created a brain-break! We found a spot in the room, turned on some Latin music, and did the 'Soca' dance. It's something IDS students love to do; it's got steps… the song itself tells you what to do, and then you just follow what the song is saying. And the purpose is PURE FUN, while giving the brain a chance to renew itself! Immediately following that brain-break, the students were able to get right back into their timed trials, and they all showed more enthusiasm for their investigative experiments!

We also spend time teaching children how to change their physiological state and refocus back to task. I empower students with the information that, "When you get up and move through specific brain-breaks, you're creating more oxygen in your brain, which helps you focus your attention and do your personal best."

Students also learn, even at this young age, to remind their teachers that they need a brain-break. It is amazing how quickly they understand that "these are things I can do to help myself be a good learner."

Parents volunteering in our classrooms often are amazed by how the brain-breaks add attention and "focus to task," rather than taking away precious time. During our break from the science experiments, when we did the Soca dance, one parent volunteer said it all, "Gosh, why didn't I get to do fun things like this when I was in school?"

A "Butterfly Release" Begins A Magical School Year

Michele Carlo, Primary Multiage Teacher, Grades 1 & 2
At IDS since 2001

At IDS, we know that if you give students wings, the new heights they can reach are limitless. That's why, on the first day of school, we share a special legend about butterflies and wishes with our multiage class of first and second graders.

Legend has it that if you make a wish on a butterfly, and then release the butterfly into the wild, your wish will come true. So, we have our students stand outside in pairs, each team carefully holding an envelope containing a live butterfly. Each child tells the butterfly a secret wish or a dream of what he or she wants to accomplish during the school year. Then, together, they release their butterflies!

A feeling of excitement and magic fills the air, as the children catapult into a new school year, figuratively rising with their butterflies toward achieving their personal goals. Throughout the year, when a child sees a butterfly in the garden, we sometimes overhear him or her exclaim, "That's my butterfly! I can tell by the color of its wings!"

When you involve children emotionally, they become highly engaged in their own learning; and as their hearts are touched, they grow spiritually and emotionally. The IDS school philosophy states, "*It is our belief that school should be interesting and even exciting... Our goal is to provide a relaxed, but stimulating atmosphere...*" This unique and fun butterfly experience sets an uplifting tone to encourage academic success and creative possibilities for our classroom every year.

Service + Cents = Sweet Success
Economics in Second Grade

Fran Ehrlich, Second Grade Teacher
At IDS since 1991

Each year the second graders of IDS successfully earn a profit for a local domestic violence center, because of the huge success of their chocolate factory.

During this teaching unit, they sell homemade chocolate lollipops to our school community. As they run their "factory," they practice real business procedures and skills, while performing a community service. By managing their chocolate factory, they have the opportunity to practice being productive, empowered citizens.

The first year, our young entrepreneurs earned a profit of $325.00. Using this figure as a goal, each class tries to improve their net gain every year. During this activity, the children make approximately 1,000 chocolate pops. They learn how to count money, advertise their product on the school's weekly T.V. show, tally orders, graph their results, check for quality control and follow work schedules.

These second graders appreciate all the support they receive from their family and friends who are their customers. They learn how to meet economic benchmarks by interacting and "living the jobs." Look out Godiva! Stiff competition is just around the corner from these entrepreneurs!

Every day is filled with "teachable" moments. We work to keep it simple, motivate the learner to learn by practicing the skills in a creative way, and always point out the "life skills" being used in each lesson.

The King of M&M's
Students get emotionally and morally connected to their lesson

Vickii Ausburn, Fourth Grade Teacher
At IDS since 2001

At IDS, teachers recognize the importance of teaching to the whole child. One gimmick we use to tap into the development of the students' moral and emotional intelligences is simulation. "The King of M&M's" is a simulation that provides the students with a hands-on experience of severe taxation, as was experienced by the colonists during early American history.

On Buccaneer Day (celebrating Tampa's NFL team), the class "King" sat with his parliament, deciding how much tax their "loyal subjects" (fellow students) should pay on various items. One set of objects that the students were taxed on was their Buccaneer gear; the more they wore, the more they were taxed. We guided the King and his Court to do this in order to teach them all about past rulers who'd made unreasonable demands upon their subjects. Almost every single person in the class was taxed, and they had to give most, if not all of their "money" (M&M's) to the King. They could see that, while his pile was getting bigger, theirs was getting smaller; and immediately, after just the first taxation was passed by the parliament, the students were chanting, "Down with the King!" They were able to empathize with the colonists through their *emotions*, and understood, through their own experience, how furious the colonists must have become toward the King of England, who was making all of these unfair tax laws. As they experienced for themselves a glimpse of such unjust acts, they were better able to discern between "fair and unfair," or "right and wrong."

The students wrote about their experience; and when they put their emotions down on paper, it was as though they'd just lived through that historical period. This simulation gave them a truer sense of themselves and greater clarity about what they feel is just and unjust. Through exercises like this, our students learn to think for themselves, and develop their emotional and moral intelligences, while learning history at the same time.

Source: Teacher Created Materials, Inc. American History Simulations. Quality Resource Book, 1993.

Student-Centered Classrooms

Lisa Hutchinson, Fourth Grade Teacher
At IDS since 1998

With all of the great brain research that has taken place over the past couple of decades, I feel that those of us who are educators today are lucky, because we have so many strategies from which to choose that can really accelerate the learning process for our students. We *study and study* cooperative learning, the integration of the multiple intelligences and KTAV, brain-based learning, and *M.O.R.E.*!

At IDS, *all of us* follow the belief that children are successful on assessments, standardized or classroom, because of the integration and implementation of multiple strategies. Having so many strategies from which to choose, allows us to tap into what works to make each individual student successful; and, in turn, we as teachers feel more successful.

When you walk into our classrooms, you might see our students working cooperatively, participating in a skit, or even singing a song to learn or practice concepts. Our classrooms are lively, energetic places where students have fun learning!

While these occurrences are typical in our school days, also typical is the traditional idea of students working solo; individual accountability, as well as being a team player, is important to our students' success. The ways in which we implement so many strategies for learning helps our students to learn better and, in turn, be more productive, well-rounded individuals.

One particular example of the success of our students comes to mind. A few years ago when our students were taking the math portion of a standardized test, we noticed one of our students thinking through one of the problems quite carefully. I walked over to see which problem he was solving. The problem had a box with an arrow pointed upward and asked what it would look like if it was turned upside down and counterclockwise. I turned to my teammates with a smile, as he took his test booklet and turned it upside down and counterclockwise. It gave me chills to see him using such a creative strategy, called "acting it out." We were assured that the time spent on the many problem-solving strategies we were teaching our students was well worth it.

We address the diverse needs of each individual student. Our approach to applying multiple strategies to foster student achievement gives me a sense of pride, and the confidence that we are meeting the challenge of fostering a society of more creative and critical thinkers.

A Student-Centered Approach to Math

Tom Bronson and Thelma Rosenberg
At IDS since 1996 and 2000

Our middle school math students probably resemble the world, with 1) those who need to be challenged because they excel in math, 2) those who are on target (meaning a grade level or two above), or 3) those with challenges in learning math. The most powerful part of our program is the flexibility to present concepts in multiple ways. We utilize novel approaches to present each concept, always teaching to the three levels of learning described above.

Traditionally, math has been a struggle for many students. We hypothesize that this is because of a *teacher-centered* approach versus a *student-centered* approach. A *teacher-centered* approach delivers the content using one or two methods and expects the students to "get it." This approach is supported by the bell-shape curve concept, which accepts success for some and failure for others.

We prefer a *student-centered* approach, focusing on finding options that will reach each student's ability to successfully grasp the concepts. Actually, we are always dialoguing about ways to capitalize on students' multiple intelligences, so that they have *multiple* ways to integrate the information.

The *teacher-centered* approach relies mainly on lecture, some classroom practice, and homework for reinforcement. On the other hand, math at IDS is treated more like learning tennis, golf, or dance. Rehearsal and repetition are honored through "practice, practice, practice," while using a plethora of strategies, including "hands-on" techniques, teamwork, technology and anything that takes into account the uniqueness of all learners.

Our approach to repetition balances novelty and routine. The goal is to ensure that everyone understands the **concepts** and develops the ability to apply **skills** to homework, tests and the real world.

Three Schools of Math: Traditional, Current and Future
Using Variety for Student Success

Don Dewey, Middle School
Integrating Technology and Math
At IDS Since 1993

In mathematics, there are often many different ways to solve the same problem. Three approaches are 1) the "old school" – use of written derivations and computations, 2) the "current school" – use of textbooks, and 3) the "future school" – use of technology tools.

At IDS, the students learn how to solve math problems using all three approaches. The reason we do this is so that each student can learn which combination of approaches works best for him or her. The benefits for students can be long-term, as they will more easily be able to adapt to any school setting once they graduate from the IDS middle school.

Adding the technology-based future approach to each math classroom introduces many students to the computer as a real "tool." Certainly, we want to know what the students know; and using computer technology allows us to find out a great deal from students whose learning styles are best supported by technology-based instruction.

Another area of math in which we use variety is concept mastery. The secret to success in understanding mathematical concepts is simple: constant practice and immediate feedback. Besides giving the students a regular routine of practice exercises to develop and reinforce their math skills around specific concepts, we also use computer websites such as *www.quizlab.com* and *www.aaamath.com* to generate a daily assessment that lets us know how each student is doing, with regard to any given assignment and all mathematical concepts. When students have difficulty with an assignment, they immediately go for individual remediation to whichever of the three math teachers suits their learning styles. This approach has worked extremely well for our middle school students, regardless of their math levels.

Having a variety of approaches and options makes it easier for us to facilitate each student's success, and allows students to keep using the learning style with which they are most comfortable.

A Random Method Supports Responsibility

Betty George, Middle School Science Teacher,
Division Leader, and Director of Studies
At IDS since 1991

Every teacher here uses a random method for calling upon students to respond to content questions. I have a draw-bag containing seat numbers and also one with little objects that represent each of the classroom teams. Some teachers use Popsicle sticks labeled with student names or small balls marked with seat numbers. Students learn quickly that when a question is posed, *anyone* in the classroom may be called upon.

Growing up, you may recall a classroom where those with answers eagerly waved their "ooh, ooh, ooh" hands in the air, while others slumped down in their seats hoping to be passed over by the teacher. You may have experienced a classroom where a select few were called upon, while other hands in the air seemed invisible to the teacher.

In our cooperative teams, our students know that, besides being responsible for themselves, they are also responsible to their teammates. When teams lean in to complete a task or answer a question, they understand that anyone may be randomly selected to represent their team. Teams work together to make sure that all four team members understand the material well enough to present their work or give their answer to the entire class.

By calling names randomly in a traditional recitation mode, the students feel like they're treated equally and are on alert to be called upon. In the team approach, they learn to develop a greater sense of responsibility to their teammates, and, by working cooperatively, every student gets the support of his or her classmates in order to master the content. In both examples, solo accountability and team accountability, a simple, systematic technique for calling on students increases time-on-task and interest in the lesson, while developing responsible learners.

George the Gorilla
...in Middle School?

Betty George, Middle School Science Teacher,
Division Leader, and Director of Studies
At IDS since 1991

I always have my students do some relaxation or positive, peaceful thinking to prepare appropriately for our science tests. We practice saying simple positive self-talk statements such as, "I am prepared for this test," or "The answers will come quickly and easily." For some students, imagining a special "peaceful place" works best, while for others simply closing their eyes and listening to specifically selected Baroque music playing softly in the background helps them to focus themselves for the test ahead. These approaches clearly honor diverse learning styles and multiple intelligences.

Another approach that we use to build a comfortable and effective testing environment is implementing novelty and fun. My science-teaching partner, Gery Morey, and I have a collection of stuffed animals in our classrooms. They serve as "table mascots" on test days and provide a special kind of comfort that even middle schoolers enjoy. A few years ago, Gery found a stuffed gorilla who says positive statements like, "You're a genius!", "That's fabulous!" and "Great Idea!" when you press his paw. Her students named him George and his positive phrases quickly became a part of our sixth grade classes on test days. Before a test, we randomly select a student from each team to press George's paw. They listen to his statement and then repeat the statements in a resounding choral response.

You might ask, "Would middle schoolers willingly do this?" In a world where students seem in such a hurry to grow up, the answer may surprise you. At first, we were doing this only in our sixth grade classes. Then, seventh and eighth graders asked Gery about George; and before we realized it, a tradition was born! Now George the Gorilla is a routine they expect before every test.

Creating a warm and friendly classroom environment is a basic goal of every teacher at IDS. We have seen the research results firsthand. When students feel comfort and safety, then they are more likely to perform better on tests. George the Gorilla and our other "test buddies" are an important part of our science classrooms, and we're glad to provide the middle schoolers with these "positively powered" stuffed animals.

Read, Write and Connect

Lynne Grigelevich, Middle School English Teacher
At IDS since 2002

Discovering the connection between young people and young adult protagonists in novels is a very powerful teaching tool. Young people face issues and challenges as they grow, and they often struggle with how to handle them. In most YA novels, the main character experiences a life lesson and eventually discovers how to make positive, healthy choices to cope with or overcome the challenge. By placing, in a student's hand, a book in which a character is "going through the same thing," a teacher gives that student validation, connection and choice.

When we explore the summer reading novel, *Freak the Mighty*, by Rodman Philbrick, we look at the different subjects tackled in this fantastic book: friendship, intelligence, family, and death; we identify the themes of the novel, or what the author is trying to convey about each of those subjects. I place four large pieces of butcher paper around the room, each one headed with one of the four subjects. In small groups, the students rotate from paper to paper, writing their own thoughts on each subject. They have the freedom to express whatever they would like to express, maintaining appropriate and respectful language. They may write personal feelings, memories, words or other thoughts that come to mind. When each group has had a chance to contribute to each subject, the students rotate again to read what others have shared.

Following a discussion on how these four subjects can mean different things to different people, I ask the students to brainstorm positive messages that would represent and characterize each of the subjects. They have the chance to create a theme of their own based on any of the subjects they choose. The only requirement is that each message be positive. Using a Kagan structure, *Round Robin*, they check each other's work for appropriateness.

Each student then receives three large rectangles of red or orange construction paper. Their job is to turn three positive messages into three bricks for a wall, our "Wall of Graffiti." When all of the bricks are completed, I collect them and, that evening, I create a brick wall around our classroom door.

The students love to see their piece of the wall, and they love reading the bricks of others. We have created a representation of a wonderful novel that incorporates both the author's ideas and the students' ideas, and that allows the students to see what they can create when they work together. Each student has expressed his or her voice, and by putting them all together, they have created something even bigger... connections to each other.

The Hook:
Planting Seeds in the Imagination

Fred Mahusay, Middle School Technology Teacher
At IDS since 2002

"Do you know someone who was on one of the planes? Did you ever meet someone who visited the Twin Towers? Have *you* ever looked down from the observation deck? What was it like? Have *you* ever visited New York?"

When students in my computer class were assigned the task of creating and designing a visual and written one-year-later reflection about September 11, 2001, they became so involved in the activity that learning word-processing and graphics software became a natural extension of their project.

Word-processing can seem tedious to many students, *except* when they're asked to describe how they feel about something as significant as September 11, 2001, how they felt on that day, or what has changed in their lives since that tragic time. At times like this, students perform and produce excellent work because they are motivated to express themselves. By my asking real world questions, I assisted students in choosing to invest in meaningful work using technology as a tool. Now, they ask me questions such as, "How do I bold the words?" or "How do I combine words and graphics?" Technology took on more value by stimulating need and desire. Student work soared in depth, length and substance.

Technology has also added relevance for our students through a "cross-curricular" approach. I often look at what the other teachers are going to teach (via their Curriculum Maps), and create assignments that augment what the students will be learning in other subject areas.

Social studies, Spanish, English, science, math and P.E. take on a new look when combined with technology classes! For example, when the Tampa Bay Buccaneers were on their way to the Superbowl, students designed databases, analyzed player stats and created brochures of San Diego that included maps, attractions and historical facts.

In my class, students are expected to live up to the following standards: 1) attitude with willingness to learn and try new ideas, 2) performance and accuracy (including technological skills, spelling, grammar and organizational skills), and 3) production that considers what makes for an attractive layout, what catches the eye. We prepare students for the standards of the world of work. What they have learned to do with and through technology is amazing!

To me, teaching is like planting healthy seeds in the forest of students' imaginations. By integrating the real world into classroom assignments, I have found that students, on their own, will tend to the technological details that make their projects come to life.

"Drawing Out" Participation in Middle School Students

Gery Morey, Middle School Science Teacher
At IDS since 1969

The word "educate" comes from a Latin word that means, "to draw out." To educate means that you see students with minds full of information and potential. To educate means to help students draw out what is already in their mind and to organize, add to and restructure that information. To educate does not mean to "push in." That is how you stuff pillows!

Students come to us full of "stuff." Our job as teachers should be to help students make sense of that stuff and integrate it with new stuff. The multitude of techniques we use at IDS allows each student to experience a variety of ways to become educated.

For example, suppose the topic being studied is photosynthesis. Students come to class with unique information about photosynthesis. They also come to class with their own unique learning styles. Now, as a teacher, I draw all of this information out of the students and guide them to reorganize it into more meaningful, higher levels of thought. Many techniques can be used to accomplish this goal.

- Solo time, such as reading the text and completing an outline, is an important piece. This gives students the opportunity to compare what they already know to new information from the text.

- Structured lab activities, such as separating chlorophyll from leaves, give students the opportunity to manipulate materials and form their thoughts.

- Cooperative lab investigations allow students to share what they know and work together to create a new procedure that would test the effect of sunlight on plants. By allowing students to create their own procedure, the teacher is drawing out what they already know and helping them to build on prior knowledge. With teams, they learn "all of us are smarter than one of us."

- Teams of four students work together to create team visuals or presentations, such as a poster that illustrates what they now know about photosynthesis, and pulls prior knowledge together into a more meaningful unit.

These are just a few of the many different techniques which help teachers truly "educate," or draw out information, while respecting the uniqueness of diverse learning styles and planning for a balance between novelty and routine.

Two Things Kids Want To Do

Heather Robinson, Middle School Science Teacher
At IDS since 2002

Two things middle schoolers seem to naturally want to do are: 1) get up and walk around, and 2) talk to their friends; so, I do all I can to keep the learning environment "child friendly" by incorporating their needs into activities that also increase student "time on task."

For example, sometimes I have the class review for an exam in the following way: first, I post five large sheets of paper around the room and write a different "test topic" on each one. Then, I divide the page into four square sections. One square section is assigned for each student team. The student teams rotate to each of the posters and every student writes on the sheet what he or she knows about that topic in their team's respective square. The teams and the squares are numbered. This makes walking and talking "legal," and they love it! They are also on task and learning!

The Kagan Cooperative Learning training makes it clear that individual accountability is also important; so the students within each team use different colored pencils, allowing everyone to easily see what each person has written. We then review, as a class, what they've learned.

When learning is experiential, the students are engaged, and therefore more likely to be focused on the topic, even when they're talking with each other. When we were studying astronomy, I decided to make our lesson about the 'Big Bang' theory more of a 'hands on' experience. I had the students go outside to the playing field and stand in a circle. Then, together, they 'exploded' by running outward from the circle, to demonstrate the 'open-universe' theory. To show the 'closed-universe' theory, the students started in a circle, ran outward, and then ran back into the circle. They returned to the classroom where they reflected on what was learned through a writing exercise, using the journal approach.

This Big Bang lesson is an example of how I try to incorporate body movement and 'hands-on' learning into every lesson. It works because we honor student diversity. Some students are kinesthetic learners; they learn best by doing, touching and moving. In fact, one of my students learns best when he is walking and talking; so now I encourage him to study this way, whenever possible.

There is a time for talking, and there is also a time for quiet, like when I'm giving instructions, describing new material and during exams. I find that when I give students what they want, they give me what I want, too – and that is their best!

Source: Kagan, Rotating Reviews

P.E. with the Brain in Mind

Coach Kathy Folen, P.E. Teacher
At IDS since 1981

There are numerous studies about the importance of physical education and its connection to learning beyond the gymnasium. We base our program on the belief that movement helps to prepare the brain for welcoming knowledge. It's exciting to finally live in an era when P.E. and physical activity are becoming more and more recognized as essential to a learning environment, both in and outside of the classroom. The old P.E. "jock" syndrome is gradually being replaced by the recognition that movement feeds the brain.

Our Physical Education program works to balance fun with skill building, as well as teamwork with varied "personalities." We use P.E. to help build self-confidence, interpersonal relationships, responsible behaviors and independence. Putting emphasis on P.E. also puts emphasis on living a healthy, active life.

A peek into any one of our Physical Education classes will be an adventure into witnessing specific cross-lateral movements and movement stations designed to strengthen the neural pathways *and* student connections to one another. Our lessons are planned with the brain in mind.

If we do our job right, we act as a great support to the classroom teacher. Examples include:

1) The continents can be reinforced with movement of seven body parts.
2) The study of planets becomes a basketball jump shot skill lesson, as students practice moving from planet to planet.

3) Rhythm and music combine with physical activity to tap into our multiple intelligences and integrate individual physical strengths in a variety of ways.

4) Kagan Cooperative games link classroom-learning strategies with skill building in our P.E. class. The ideas are limitless. The IDSers enjoy P.E. The teachers love to have us integrate their curriculum into our P.E. time; and I love to create exciting lessons – always keeping the brain in mind.

What Will Stay With Them Their Whole Lives?

Tom McColley, Music Specialist
At IDS since 1994

When planning lessons, it is important to start by thinking about what you want the students to know at the end, and working backwards from there. That is different than testing. In most testing situations, there are minimal standards that students ought to know, and often people end up teaching to those minimal standards.

I mean it in more of a philosophical way. When you have children who go from Pre-K through eighth grade, what do you want them to know about music when they finish? What will stay with them for their whole lives? In fact, I ask myself, "Which things about music are going to transform their lives?"

Great music has the power to help students transcend everyday musical trends. When you introduce four or five-year olds to Beethoven, they think it's so cool to learn the stories and hear the music. They are usually without preconceived notions.

We teach them jazz and folk music, as well as other styles, and then have the students create the music and perform it. At times, they even build instruments.

Almost every person you meet is passionate about some type of music; often what that means is that they're passionate about their prejudices. We want people to have a bigger vision of what music is and what music can be. With younger kids, it's easy because they're free of so many of the typical musical prejudices. In middle school, music is more than just music. It's image. It's who's cool and who's not.

We've been able to do things at IDS that really help the kids "stretch out" musically, so that they reach beyond what they had previously thought possible for themselves.

Last year, every single IDS middle school student composed at least one piece of original music, and one student even recorded an entire CD of his music.

We listened to dozens of examples of musical styles, ranging from traditional songs to experimental multi-media creations, and everything in between. All of the students created something, which means that they mastered the basics of the technology and they took a chance by saying, "These ideas are my musical ideas and I'm going to bring them to life using the computer and keyboard."

Each student also burned a CD of his or her musical piece. Many students performed at concerts that we held at IDS, where audience members could go up and listen to the students' compositions. It was magnificent *and* memorable, because everybody was creating. They did it, while learning the process of how creative artists work.

These experiences with music can affect them for life. Music changes people's lives. It always has and always will.

Lesson Plan Generator

Kim Rostick, Technology Specialist
At IDS since 2002

After teaching for eight years, receiving National Board Certification and becoming a workshop addict, I arrived at IDS and found so much more to learn. One of the great influences on me, both personally and professionally, has been my learning to consider the many aspects of a brain-friendly philosophy when creating my lesson plans.

The IDS Lesson Plan Generator (LPG) is a web-based computer program on our school's network, which consolidates exemplary teaching practices into a user-friendly framework. This ensures that we, as a faculty, are consistent in our application of maximizing student success. The LPG provides a model for the many academic options available to me when designing a lesson. By adding the big "V" for variety, with a dash of novelty and routine, I can be certain before teaching a lesson that I am reaching all of the children. By attending to all learning styles, and considering their respective intake and processing differences, as well as behavioral styles, I can optimize my lessons. This process also helps me clarify my own thinking and the implementation of the lesson. Later, I use the LPG to refine and reflect on future lessons.

I am grateful to our Directors of Study who had the vision to marry the philosophy, which we rehearse in training, to actual practical teacher-student connections. Reflecting on good teaching daily through the LPG has tightened my lessons.

Making it a habit, like anything, takes practice and persistence. The LPG process can be lengthy and requires a deeper examination of what, why and how I teach. After this mental workout, I feel fit, firm and functional as an educator.

The teachers at IDS have a high standard of excellence and the LPG helps us maintain the goal of making every child shine.

Disabilities Day for Eighth Grade

Coach Jeff Smith
At IDS since 2000

At IDS, students are taught to recognize, respect and appreciate the differences between themselves and others. On one particular day, we had the eighth graders meet in the gym, and we drew names out of a hat; then, each person was randomly given a "disability" and a task to perform.

They might have been wheelchair-bound, missing a limb, blind or partially blind. Some students were paired up and others were on their own.

One of the tasks was to set a table for four. Another was to make a peanut butter and jelly sandwich. These were challenging assignments, especially for the students who had to pretend they were missing an arm or hand. While some used their mouths, others used their feet. All of the students really got into the experience.

The goal of this lesson was for students to learn to appreciate what they *do* have, while also respecting the challenges that some people must overcome just to be able to function in society.

There is one story that will always stay with me. The activity started with students pairing up and drawing a picture of their partners. Then, they each had to find a new partner, who they had to describe and explain their picture to without showing them. Finally, based solely on this descriptive explanation, their new partner had to draw what they had heard.

We had one boy who was learning what it was like to have only one arm. Since his partner was blind, he chose to explain to her what his picture looked like by taking her finger with his one hand and tracing the picture. By repeating this a few times, she was eventually able to draw it.

With a greater awareness of how others experience life's challenges, I watched as students displayed acceptance and respect for diversity. Using simulation instead of lecture, I feel we helped students develop sensitivity and an appreciation for life.

Give the Students What They Want

Coach Jeff Smith
At IDS since 2000

In our middle school, we have a lunchtime fitness program called "Intramurals." Students participate in activities, both cooperative and competitive, for about 15 to 20 minutes before each lunch period. Initially, we had challenges because some of the students preferred to do other things with their time.

Seventh and eighth-graders had a choice of yoga, field games, gym games or aerobics. Those participating in aerobics were getting tired of it; they wanted to do something else.

Brainstorming ideas with my students, I listened to their ideas. Students had guidelines, as there were space challenges and goals that needed to be met. But this opportunity gave them ownership with the outcome and was another chance to work together as a team.

Our brainstorming session created a new activity at IDS called "Walk and Talk." In a creative way, it met both the students' desire to talk and carry on conversations with friends and teachers, and the school goals of 20 minutes of sustained physical activity and socialization.

Now we have "Walk and Talk," along with other options. It is going really well. I'm sure it will change again, at some point; but the key is to listen to what the students want. Working together within guidelines that gave students ownership with responsible options resulted in a successful, cooperative decision-making model.

Group Dynamics- Making Connections:

Personal and Professional Growth for Kids!

Class Meetings for 'Pre-K'ers

Karen Jankowski, Pre-K
Primary Co-Division Leader and Admissions Assistant
At IDS since 1979

Setting boundaries in a way that feels safe and friendly to the children is basic to a successful classroom environment. At the beginning of the year, teachers orchestrate a "class meeting." During this meeting, we talk about "class values."

We even ask our youngest Pre-K students, "How can we stay safe in our classroom?" and "How can we help each other feel important in our classroom?" The teacher facilitates this brainstorm session by positively rewording the comments and reflecting on their meaning.

These "values" become rules for the students to live by every day. We begin reinforcing values in the classroom immediately. When students get overly excited or they need reminders, the teacher points out the class values, which are "owned" by the class because they wrote them.

Positive Phrasing Makes Coaching More Palatable

Mrs. Michelle Robson, Pre-K Teacher
At IDS since 2001

The environment here is so positive, largely because people speak in positive ways. I notice the difference when I go elsewhere and I hear negative phrasing.

With the uplifting tone that's set here, it's easier to coach people, and to receive coaching; it's even easier to work together. I think that giving people the opportunity to learn positive phrasing sets the groundwork for a great school. We focus on what we want people to know or do, even when we ask questions.

Someone Understands My Child!
Appreciating, Accepting, Accommodating

Mrs. Michelle Robson, Pre-K Teacher
At IDS since 2001

My son is very active and had some challenges in pre-school. Teachers would get frustrated when he would wiggle in circle time and during story time. I tried to help by offering to buy a larger circle-time rug! I knew, though, that my three-year old was still going to continually move about; he just needed to learn to respect his classmates' personal space.

Then, I brought him to IDS. During the first week of school, Mrs. L, his kindergarten teacher, said to me, "Your son 'lives' in an auditory-kinesthetic world. He loves to answer questions during circle time. He simply needs to move around more than other children, so we just scoot him back to give him a little more room."

I threw my hands up, "Someone finally gets my child!" I was so relieved. Because of the variety in teaching methods that stretch and match learning styles, his needs were finally understood and accommodated. That began my love affair with IDS and was the main reason I chose to return to teaching after being a 'stay at home' mom.

Teachers at IDS are trained to value the importance of appreciating, accepting and accommodating each student's modalities, even in Pre-K. Varied learning styles have made all the difference for so many, including my son.

Mrs. Harrison's Links Create a Classroom Community

Jean Harrison, Kindergarten Teacher
At IDS since 1998

To me, classroom management is love! It's how the children feel when they're there. Everything is positive. For example, to reinforce positive student behavior, we hang paper links from our ceiling, and whenever my class does something that goes above and beyond as a community or as a classroom family, links are added.

If people are walking and someone remarks to our class, "What a nice class this is, Mrs. Harrison," then they get a link. Links are also given for working well in class together, or when they help someone else outside of our class. Giving service to others is the underlying message.

It takes about 75 links to get to the floor. We save links for extra special occasions. The students are really eager to watch their links grow in numbers. It's novelty for them because it's usually a surprise when they receive one, and a goal they proudly work to achieve. In January, the links reached the ground, and a performance by my mother and father, who are professional clowns, was the reward for reaching their goal!

I have to work hard to remember to give links because behavior that was good in the beginning is now part of our everyday expectations. So you see, we're constantly raising the bar, in community interaction, as well as in our academic program.

For example, today a student fell, and his peers stopped and asked, "Are you okay?" At the beginning of the year, I would have given a link for that; but this time a link wasn't even expected. Now, that kind of caring behavior just happens naturally. At IDS, the children have been raised in a very positive, loving way. With the "links" approach, we build group support and reinforce learning how to take care of each other.

One day, the phone rang while my kids were sitting on the floor during circle time, and I really had to answer it. It was a parent and the students must have known it was important. From my voice, they could probably tell something was wrong. I was talking on the phone for a few minutes when all of a sudden it dawned on me, "Look what the children are doing." I turned around and they were just sitting there. They got it! That was a 4-link day. It brought tears to my eyes that they would wait so patiently, especially since they are active kindergarteners.

For their next reward, my dog is coming to learn with us for a day. Scooby Doo is his name, and the kids are so excited! It's just fun little stuff like that which turns routine tasks into novelty and makes their day.

Zeroing Into EQ

Kim Fowler, First Grade Teacher
At IDS since 1998

As an IDS educator, my students' emotional intelligence, or EQ, is a priority. That means making sure the children feel safe, cared for and loved at all times. Emotional intelligence seems to be at the foundation of successful learning. It is paramount that my students know that I am aware of what they're feeling, when they're feeling it.

For example, I created a "How Do You Feel? Mobile." At the top is a large heart, entitled "How Do You Feel?" Hanging below are tags with "emotion" labels like HAPPY, SAD, PEACEFUL, ANGRY and others. Each child uses a clothespin with his or her name on it to clip on the tag that represents how he or she is feeling at anytime throughout the day. This hands-on strategy immediately helps me tune in to the students' individual emotions and better understand their behavior.

For instance, imagine that "Kristie" had clipped her clothespin to "HAPPY" earlier in the morning. Yet after snack time, she marches in and moves it to "ANGRY." That gives me an opportunity to pull Kristie aside privately and use our verbal skills to uncover her agenda, "Is there something you want to talk about or tell me? How can I help?" Most of the time, the child is all too ready to talk, which helps solve small issues before they become large ones.

I use various tools and approaches to open up and maintain the lines of communication between the students and myself. The greater awareness I have of the children's needs, especially their emotional needs, the better I'm able to create an ideal academic learning environment for them.

That "special connection" involves knowing who they are outside of school, too. For example, I once had a student who was having challenges in class, and I met with his father. We sorted things out. The next year, the father passed away. Even though the boy was in a new grade level, I went to the funeral. Noticing me, the boy ran up and embraced me, saying, "I can't believe you came!" I thought, "Of course I came. I care about you." Now, years later, he hugs me whenever he sees me.

If asked how I create lasting connections with my students, four things come to mind:

Listen: Really give students your full attention. Your eyes and body language will let them know that you genuinely care about what they're telling or asking you.

Inquire: Ask them questions that show you are interested in them and their lives: "What do you do for fun?" or "How was your soccer game last weekend?"

Play: Joining in with what is fun to them secures instant respect. Try joining in at whatever they may do during "down time."

Kneel to their level: Use eye contact that sparkles, along with a smile that says, "You're number one at this moment."

Self-Esteem is Strongly Correlated with Learning

Jaclyn Kanarish, Primary Multiage, Grades 1 & 2
An IDS Resident, 2002-2003

The students at IDS are excited to come to school because the teachers and administration make sure that their environment feels inviting, as well as exciting. Focusing on what makes an individual special is what I will always remember from my internship, and I remember the lesson that strongly influenced my approach to working with children.

During the Spring of 2002, as an intern in first grade, I learned about KOW, or "Kid Of the Week." I observed Kim Fowler, my cooperating teacher, walk around the room creating a "mind map" of a student. We will pretend her name was Sara. Mrs. Fowler wrote Sara's name in a circle in the center of the whiteboard, and then interviewed students in the class to find out what they thought was special about her. Students volunteered ideas, showing at an early age how to appreciate each other.

As each child shared special thoughts about Sara, Kim noted his or her comments on the page. Then she drew a line from the comment to Sara's name in the center circle, until all of the children had an opportunity to participate in the project. Later on, each student colored a page and wrote letters of appreciation for Sara as part of their writing assignment, to be included in a book designed just to make Sara feel special.

My heart began to melt as I observed Mrs. Fowler and the first grade students. "Every classroom could be like this," I thought. The "Kid Of the Week" experience may only happen once in a lifetime for a student, but the boost in self-esteem will last forever.

Self-Confidence: It's Essential!

Judy Sobel, Third Grade Teacher
At IDS since 1988

I work to make my classroom a very nurturing environment. When students come into my room, I want them to dance into the room; I want them to feel happy and relaxed. I greet them as they come in, call them by name, let them know how happy I am that they're there. I want them to feel safe enough to make mistakes and to learn from them.

I give my students the same dignity and respect that I want from them, so that each feels valued. I give them a feeling that they can do just about anything they want to do, and they're not limited by what happened last year or by what other people think about them. I know that they have the ability to soar, and I'm there to help them reach their greatest heights. It's very important that they know that I think they can do it. They believe me and then it seems to come to fruition. I am told that my deep belief in the great potential for each child is like massaging each heart so that it beats with confidence.

I learned this at a very early age when diagnosed with polio and admitted into an isolation hospital. I was sure I was going to die. While waiting for my turn to be examined, I saw a four-year old dancing in the hallway. The nurse noticed my solemn mood and pointed to the little boy, as she said with confidence, "Everyone does that when they leave here. After 21 days, you will too."

The kind nurse reversed my whole belief in what could be, and indeed, I recovered in 21 days from polio. I guess that is what I strive to do for my students every day.

Teaching with Enthusiasm!
An Interview with Amy Lewis

Amy Lewis, Fifth Grade Teacher
Resident and Intern 2000-2002

Q: What do you most enjoy about teaching?
Amy: I love children. I enjoy watching them grow, seeing them progress, witnessing their development in so many areas. Children are gifts to this world, and I get to be a part of their lives. It is wonderful to learn about each individual's special personality and what makes him or her tick. They are all unique, and I enjoy being able to peek into their minds and help them learn. What a fabulous way to spend my day!

Q: What do you do well?
Amy: I'm able to put enthusiasm into my lessons. I try to keep the students entertained enough to pay attention and focus on the learning opportunities. In school, I was a cheerleader, and some of that "cheering" and "encouragement" carries over to my teaching. I try to use my arms, voice and body motions to keep them interested. It's almost like being an actress.

Q: What have you learned from your experience at IDS?
Amy: I've studied, along with our faculty, the section from the *M.O.R.E. Approach*, on ways to use body language with purpose, including how and when to lean in, use open arms, and varied facial expressions to capture students' attention. My intention is to stimulate the students' interest and guide their focus toward the topics at hand. I also use my voice to vary Volume, Intensity, Pause, and Speed. We call that our *VIPS*, which is also part of the *M.O.R.E. Approach*.

We also have training reminders, called the "BIG V for Variety," ensuring that we vary our presentations always using KTAV (Kinesthetic, Tactual, Auditory and Visual). I even practice matching my words to my tonality and gestures during presentations. If my delivery is in a regular, even talking voice, without gestures or movements, I most likely would lose my students to "mini-vacations."

Q: What is the best part of being a teacher?
Amy: It's energizing for me to see the students respond to me positively. I can see interest in their eyes as they lean in to listen and grasp the message being taught! I work to create a brain-friendly learning environment. Teaching this way is just fun!

A Middle School Community: Expectations, Support & Service

Barbara Grady, Middle School Social Studies Teacher
At IDS since 1989

There are many things we do to create a feeling of community in middle school that tap into the intellectual, physical, social and emotional development of that delicate age. Some examples include: 1) An in-school retreat, 2) faculty-facilitated advisory groups, and 3) special field trips.

EXPECTATIONS
In the beginning of the year, the middle school has an in-school retreat, where all of the teachers and students spend time together doing team-building activities and going over school rules and expectations. We do a lot of

role-playing, demonstrating behavior that would be considered non-examples, as well as what would be appropriate. The middle schoolers really get a kick out of watching the teachers and headmaster misbehave! Then, of course, we discuss and model appropriate behavior, setting high expectations.

This retreat sets the tone for the year to transition our sixth graders into the middle school, as well as orient new students who learn our expectations *right from the beginning*. The retreat contributes greatly to unifying the middle school community.

SERVICE AND SUPPORT

Throughout the year, all of the middle school teachers serve as advisory leaders, and all of our students participate in Multi-Age advisory groups. The teachers team up in pairs to assist each advisory group. We meet together in our group once a week for about half an hour. During that time, we talk about various topics of interest or of concern to the students. Examples include any problems they might be having with course work, in relationships or other areas of concern. They also bond by sharing about themselves; the older students learn by giving advice to the younger middle schoolers.

We also participate in activities together, like giving service back to the community. This week, my group spent the morning at Tampa General Hospital in the children's ward. In the afternoon, we went to Lake Park and cleaned up. Each advisory group did something different. In fact, a local newspaper wrote an article about our volunteerism and our strong community service focus.

NEW HORIZONS

At the end of every year, the students go on field trips. The sixth graders go to Pathfinders, which is a science team-building program in Bradenton, Florida; the seventh graders cross the state lines to go backpacking in the mountains; and the eighth graders go with me to Washington D.C. and Williamsburg. The students are all encouraged to participate in the field trips and really look forward to them. Each trip correlates to academic standards and designated learning benchmarks.

Meaningful travel activities that connect to the curriculum help to create a special feeling of community, where middle schoolers can express themselves and bond with each other, as well as with their teachers. This truly creates powerful connections that cross over to classroom success.

To Flex or to Flex?

Gery Morey, Middle School Science Teacher
At IDS since 1969

Teaching is about connecting just the right elements in just the right way, like putting together a stained-glass window. Just like a stained glass window is made up of many different-colored, different-shaped pieces of glass, the classroom is composed of many different children with individual needs and unique situations.

To effectively meet this wide range of needs and situations, I must always be ready to flex, in order to help the students make connections that are lasting and meaningful. Sometimes, my focus is to keep the students on-task, so they can complete their lessons successfully. Other times, my focus shifts to a child who needs to have his or her birthday recognized; so the lesson is put on hold while the class celebrates with a song and perhaps a treat.

Even though the celebration takes time, the students return more focused and on-task than they would have been if the opportunity to celebrate had been denied.

Each day in the classroom is made up of many different events, some planned and some spontaneous. For example, tight lesson plans must be prepared for each period. However, I must be willing to change them in a heartbeat when a fire drill or student council announcement interrupts the class. As a teacher, I must enforce clear rules regularly and fairly. At the same time, I must also be willing to bend and even break the rules for certain unexpected situations.

As a teacher, I must be willing and able to flow easily from one approach to another or combine parts to create a whole, just like that stained-glass window. Having a wide range of methods and a comfortable attitude about applying them empowers me to make connections come alive for all students.

Making Connections with Middle School Students

Amy Ragg-Smith, Middle School English Teacher, Former IDS student; Teacher at IDS since 2002

At IDS, the English teachers learn a lot about the students from their Writer's Notebooks (WNB), which are a combination of a journal and a response to their reading. The WNB becomes their safe-place to write about anything and everything, without fear of being judged.

The WNB is also a place for them to communicate with their teachers. They can ask us questions, and we will answer them. They tell us, through writing, whatever seems important to them. It is a place where they can be completely honest. Each Writer's Notebook ends up being a unique reflection of the student author. It is actually quite a beautiful tool for them to use.

We make the WNB a priority. The students are required to write three entries per week. We (the English teachers) have the privilege to read them every week and respond accordingly.

Because we connect with the students on such a personal level, through their Writer's Notebooks, we create an opportunity for them to come to us to talk, and for us to get to know them as human beings, which is an incredibly important part of a true learning environment. This frees 'brain space' for learning academic subjects, because their personal needs are attended to, respected and valued.

Art from the Heart

Debbie Kerr and Susan Bossard, Art Teachers
At IDS since 1998 and 1996

Kids are "naturals" at art. Put out some markers, scraps and glue on the tables, turn loose a few children, and would-be Picassos appear to blossom right before your eyes, even before any directions are given!

How can this uninhibited creative energy be encouraged, nurtured and guided into a lifelong love of the visual arts? That is what an art teacher does – that is our calling. As with any kind of educational experience, we teachers proudly work to instill our students with the confidence to take risks and enjoy the creative process. Most importantly, an art teacher helps students realize that they have creative potential and that they can use that potential to improve the quality of their lives. We are grateful to authors like Eric Jensen, author of *Arts with the Brain in Mind*, whose work validates the role the arts play in increasing "brain power" and success in school.

Because we encourage children to take risks, those who might think that they have little artistic ability soon feel comfortable experimenting with the materials. The fun of using those materials reawakens their senses, so that students can effortlessly absorb the information being shared, knowing that they can express themselves more freely in a supportive atmosphere.

Behavioral Lessons:

Social, Emotional and Academic

Find a Way to Connect

Cynthia Brown, Kindergarten
At IDS since 1999

It was my first year teaching. I was 22 and felt brand new, just like a rookie in the big leagues. On top of it, I had a large fourth grade class. One little boy who came to my classroom had some real challenges. Most people who knew him seemed to have a lot of preconceived notions, which they delighted in sharing with me. The bottom line was, "Watch out. Here comes trouble."

I thought, "What can I do? What can I possibly do that other highly effective, seasoned teachers with experience might do?"

I quickly learned he did not like to have the spotlight cast upon him, like telling him in front of the class, "Oh, you're doing such a *great* job!" Some kids thrive on that. He didn't; so I very privately let this boy know I appreciated him and his accomplishments, with quiet comments to him, a little smile and/or a pat on the back. Gradually, I began to penetrate the wall of his "tough guy" image.

I also encouraged his every effort. I focused on helping him find meaningful connections to his work. I invested time in him, and by the end of the year, he had transformed into a more open learner, willing to accept help.

That year opened up his world and became the foundation for the next year, which proved to be a good one for him, both academically and socially. What a triumph!

His anger, volatility and deep desire to hide any inadequacies gave me an opportunity, as a new teacher, to stretch and apply all I had learned in college to the "real world." Working with him was a turning point for me! I learned that, sometimes, our toughest challenges give us our greatest growth. This experience gave me the confidence to know that, with insight, effort, love and determination, I could really reach all of my students. Still today, that gives me a sense of both pride and accomplishment.

Who's the Expert?

Jean Harrison, Kindergarten Teacher
At IDS since 1998

My best job in the classroom is to facilitate learning. The children bring up what they need and I help them meet their needs.

The children know that I am only one of the resources for them in the classroom. They learn to value classmates as resources, as well as the teacher.

We have an "expert" chart posted in the room. We discover who's an expert at tying shoes, who's an expert in reading, who's an expert at kickball, etc.

If a student comes to me for help, I often say, "Who's the expert? Please go check the chart." Or, "You know who can tie shoes; go ask them." This makes the other children feel empowered; they are helping to run the classroom. It's not just my classroom; it's *our* classroom. In fact, there's a sense that the kids run the classroom.

Some of the other "experts" are writing, reading, monkey bars, artists… you see, not all areas of "expertise" have to do with inside the classroom. We have soccer experts, baseball experts, and so on; so they know who to go to if they need the rules clarified. There are even "good friend" experts and "playing fair" experts who are natural problem solvers. We have a lot of different kinds of experts in the classroom.

It's the same among our staff. This is the best school that I have ever worked at in my entire life, and I've worked at quite a few. It's because every teacher, I think, feels the same way: we're not the "big bosses." We're here to work together and make the world better, and that's what I want to do here in kindergarten. I want them to learn to like themselves, like others, and feel comfortable tapping into others' talents for help when needed. And if they can do all that, they'll feel like they can do anything.

Stop, Count to Ten and Make a Good Choice

Debi Brockmeyer, First Grade Teacher
Primary Co-Division Leader
At IDS since 1981

I have a little sign up in my classroom that says, "They may forget what you said. They'll always remember how you made them feel." I hope that they will remember many of the things that are taught in class. Everything else, though, will blossom if you can give the children the feeling that learning is fun and the confidence to say, "I can do it; I'm capable; I like school; I like my teacher; my teacher is here to help me." When children feel good about themselves, then they feel more secure about learning, which hopefully sets the stage to empower them to grow into lifelong learners.

Although every child is special, every child is susceptible to challenges that life throws at him or her. This was the case of a little boy in my class. Life had thrown him a huge family challenge and he was confused about how to handle it. He was unhappy, upset, frustrated and frightened. These worries colored everything he did. He decided that striking out at others would be a way to release his anger and gain the attention he so desperately needed. Unfortunately, this method gave him more heartache, as his friends began to keep their distance and his teachers worried that someone might get hurt.

Finding ways to help him cope with this anger became a mission for his teachers, parents and the administration. We began by explaining to him that the brain was geared long ago to survive, or in this case, to strike out, when feeling fear or anger. We discussed that, if he gave his brain the time to think first, he could make a better decision.

When he recognized an angry feeling coming on, he was to practice this thought: "Stop, count to ten and make a good choice." He was learning how to both understand and control anger.

We practiced it with him, and the other children, many times in a role playing game. With gentle reminders, he was able to use this method, thus enabling him to keep the friendships he so needed. Taking extra time to talk with him one-on-one helped him to feel he could count on our support.

When he was especially angry, a trip to see our headmaster usually meant help and/or consistent consequences. We use "restitution," where students get the opportunity to contribute back the respect taken away from inappropriate behavioral choices. Another option was to hold meetings with the parents and the child together. This gave him another avenue to gain the attention he was seeking from them and put everyone on the same "page" regarding expectations for appropriate behavior.

Working as a team to support this young fellow, while showing him that there are *always* options to solving a problem, made all the difference. He was on the road to understanding and eventually, we reached him! That was worth all of the effort. Consistency, caring and commitment to the child's success turned a problem into a happy ending.

Bridging the Gap
Combining Emotional Well-Being with Academic Focus

Pennie Collins and Jeanne Rivera, Third Grade Teachers
At IDS since 1999 and 1997

We had a little girl whose mom was pregnant. Just as we were leaving to go to music class, she came up to us and asked, "Can I call my mommy?"

Her eyes revealed her mind's true concern. She had been experiencing a period of challenges being separated from her mom. We continued to encourage her and assure her that her Mom was alright.

She replied, "I miss her. I just want to tell her I love her."

We glanced up at the clock and then looked back at the worried little face and said, "You can make a quick call and say, 'I miss you. I love you. I only have a second."

Here was a child who had the belief that she needed to talk to her mom. It's just where she was. How could we expect her to move on and focus her attention somewhere else? By allowing her to meet her emotional needs, she was able to get much more out of the rest of her day. Having telephones in our rooms increase our options for communication at these critical times.

Whatever the situation, it seems to boil down to balancing real world needs with students' academic expectations. The focus of being a teacher here at IDS is twofold: sustain a caring and fun learning environment, while covering curriculum that prepares students to leave with the advanced skills and strategies that they need for their futures.

A Bully Thing

Judy Sobel, Third Grade Teacher
At IDS since 1988

After school at the "extended day" program, a boy went home crying and told his mom that he felt embarrassed because, even though he was bigger than the rest of the kids, a little guy was picking on him and hit him.

His mother told him never to hit; but *he* felt that it had made him look bad to allow a little guy to bully him. He came to me and told me about everything that had happened.

I did not quite know how to handle this "bully situation," so I asked our headmaster for assistance. She gave me a chart from Dr. Michele Borba's *Moral Intelligences* book, which I could use in the classroom.

I reviewed the chart with him and together we decided what kind of behavior this little guy had displayed. Then, I reviewed the concepts relating to *moral intelligences* with the entire class. As the students began to recognize how they influence one another and the behavioral options they have available to them, I immediately saw the instances of bullying decrease.

It was like magic. Kids can be mean, but given the knowledge and opportunity to use a problem-solving approach, they really get it... that is, until the next time, and then we start all over again! Each time, though, it gets easier. With the proper coaching, they really do get it.

Source: www.moralintelligence.com

A Five-Year Old Teaches Dignity and Respect

Vickii Ausburn, Fourth Grade Teacher
At IDS since 2001

My own children attend IDS. We had a couple of days off this past week and we were at home. The children in the neighborhood gravitated to our house to play. As they were playing different games, my five-year old, Quinn, walked up to the girls, who were playing checkers on a huge checker board. One of the girls was in third grade and the other was in fourth.

When one girl said something to the other using a negative tone, he looked directly at her and said, "Well, with that tone, you might need to work on your dignity and respect." I just listened and kept very quiet; that was his moment.

The girls just looked up at him as if they were wondering, "Hmmm... what should we do?" I think they thought it was cute that a five-year old was using very big words.

He then continued, addressing the 'offender': "When you say something like that *next* time, you might want to say it a little bit differently; and that way, she may say something nice back to you."

My five-year old is living in a school environment where, from a young age, the children hear how dignity and respect "sound" and know that it's an important part of creating a secure and safe learning environment.

It is so important to me that my son understands that having "dignity and respect" means thinking of others as well as oneself, in the way you talk and the way you interact. At a young age, he also understands what it means to speak to people in a way that is courteous and kind. Positive modeling pays off! I thank my colleagues for giving him this gift.

Tapping In

Lisa Hutchinson, Fourth Grade Teacher
At IDS since 1998

At IDS, we create classrooms that are student-centered. My belief is that at the heart of a great curriculum is a teacher's connection to his or her students. Teachers attending to the academic, social, and emotional needs of their students make connections with their students.

How do we do this? **LISTEN** to our students with sincerity. And think about: What makes him giggle? What is she passionate about? What makes him proud? Once we've tapped into what makes a child feel special that's what we "go with" to make our students feel valued.

One of my behaviorally challenged students often spoke of how much he loved dogs, especially his own. I grabbed onto his favorite topic and I made a point to ask him about his dog. I then ordered books about dogs for our classroom library and brought them to his attention. That did it! We immediately connected! He loved the books and knew that I cared about him as a person. From then on, cooperation was easier, even in his toughest moments!

Understanding Learning Styles Assists in Test Preparations

Betty George, Middle School Science Teacher,
Division Leader, and Director of Studies
At IDS since 1991

A few years ago, I had a sixth-grader who would always come to me at lunchtime to prepare before a science test. This handsome young man was an accomplished athlete with a winning smile. For him, preparing for the test meant that we would walk and talk, because he is a kinesthetic and auditory learner. This means he needs to be moving, thinking and talking, all at the same time. We would walk around outside or in the classroom while reviewing orally for the test. Whenever we had concrete models to reinforce a concept, I would be sure that there were "hands on" opportunities, too, for kinesthetic learners like him. Sometimes, we made props or drew pictures to help him grasp the information.

This student could often demonstrate his understanding of a concept orally, but then might have difficulty expressing that understanding on a written test. During our middle school faculty sessions, we discussed the best ways to meet his needs for testing. For subject areas where he had his greatest challenges, we decided to work one-on-one with him, reading tests orally and allowing him to respond orally, as well.

Now he is able to prepare for tests on his own. By understanding his own learning style, and knowing what to do to meet his own needs, he is able to succeed with school exams. I was so proud to hear of his performance on a high school entrance test, and happy to know that he will take some practical self-knowledge with him when he leaves IDS!

Getting Middle School Students Organized

Barbara Grady, Middle School Social Studies Teacher
At IDS since 1989

*"Mrs. Grady, thanks for helping me get organized.
It's made high school a lot easier."*
– A typical quote from IDS alumni

If students are organized, they'll more easily find success. So, one of the first things the middle school teachers at IDS do is teach the students how to create a notebook system. By keeping their schoolwork and homework well organized in their notebooks, it frees up their minds to focus on the important task at hand – learning!

I find that students who are well-organized are usually the ones who have consistently higher grades. I teach the students that, "When your lockers and your backpacks are organized and neat, your thinking is more that way, too."

There is a place for every sheet of paper, even if it means discard it in "File 13."

For some students, this comes easily; for others, this is a major challenge, depending on how they come "wired." With practice and a sense of purpose, I believe all students can master basic organizational skills. Because I believe it, and I set those expectations, most students amaze even themselves. By the time they leave eighth grade, they've got it.

I also meet with parents whose children have organizational challenges. I always say, "When you get home today, I want your child to totally clean up his (or her) room – every drawer, every closet, and under the bed. Clean it perfectly, so he (or she) feels the sense of accomplishment of a new beginning."

When the students start to slip into old habits, I remind them that this is preparation for high school, and together we're going to be sure that they're ready, again reestablishing those high expectations.

We even hold a "Breakfast Club," where those middle schoolers needing support and help in prioritizing get a fresh start every day by ensuring that every class notebook is in proper order and all assignments are completed. It amazes me how often completed work sits in backpacks and lockers, needing that next step: "Turn your work in to the teacher." If you understand that middle school is a time of hormonal turbulence, staying organized is a big deal.

Thus, we prepare our students to understand that organization is an essential habit for getting good grades now, and for creating success in the future – both in high school and for the rest of their lives.

Incomplete Assignments?
A Student is Crying Out for Help

Michael J. Vokoun, Middle School English Teacher
At IDS since 1997

Students who choose not to complete their work are signaling the teacher for help. Even though they may be unaware that they are doing so, these students are shooting off giant red flares into the air asking for help.

One of my students, who I will call Robert, had slowly but surely been falling behind in his English work, and during this particular week, his world of madly spinning plates came crashing down upon him. Robert always worked hard in English class. He participated well and usually had wonderful insights. However, Robert had trouble with work outside of class.

Though I had been keeping the parents and the middle school director of studies well informed about what Robert had been completing, promising to complete, or completely "forgetting" to complete, the time had come for an intervention: a teacher/student/parent conference.

When Robert and his dad came in, the three of us went to the main office to discuss how we could help him. First, we took time to write down all of the English work that Robert still needed to complete. We spoke about the challenges to complete that work at home and brainstormed ways that Robert could change his at-home habits, as well as how Robert's parents could help.

During the conversation, we also found out that other classes were also an organizational challenge. It turned out that Robert was taking his agenda to class; but instead of writing down his assignments, he was leaving it blank. The disorganization made Robert confused about when a

Spanish quiz was going to occur, as well as when a large science study sheet was due. He needed help in planning his study time, as well as balancing English, social studies, math, science, Spanish, and computer class assignments.

Together with his dad, we set up a schedule that included much more work at home, as well as concentrated time with me after school. We set deadlines with a check-off list of what was due when. This allowed everyone to keep current with Robert's progress. At the end of the meeting, Robert promised to complete his work; but Robert had made promises before. I left him with the saying: "Actions speak louder than words."

It took time to build sufficient momentum through planning, encouragement and diligently holding him accountable for his agreed upon workload. Eventually, Robert was able to keep current in his other classes, while also making up the work in English class; and he did it in a positive context of solving challenges for his own success.

When student actions warrant it, teachers, parents and administrators can work with them individually to make a plan for their success! Does each student deserve that? I think so.

Positive Phrasing

Señora Sonia Morgan and Señorita Lizette Geisler
Spanish Teachers
At IDS since 2002 and 2000

People respond differently when we phrase things positively. When a child is told, "Don't stand on the chair," the focus is on what is wrong, rather than on what you want to happen. If he hears, "Stay on the floor," or "Put your feet on the floor," then attention is directed to "Feet on the floor." By telling a child what you don't want, an opportunity is missed to provide a picture of what you *do* want. To help students respond to you in a positive manner, it is important to focus their attention on what you want them to know or do.

All of the teachers and staff at IDS practice using positive phrasing to communicate with each other and with their students. "No talking" or "Don't forget your homework" are now, "Please focus your attention on the group" or "Remember to complete your homework."

Robert Marquez, the facilities manager, uses positive phrasing, too. People were walking on the grass and it was getting ruined. In most instances, the sign would say, "Don't step on the grass." Instead, Robert created a new sign that reads: "Please walk on the sidewalk. Let the grass grow." It worked! The grass is green and growing.

P.P. and Coaching
Keeping Students On Task By Using Positive Phrasing

Barbara McBride, Music Specialist
At IDS since 2002

When I first came here, I thought I was such a positive person, and in other schools, compared to other people, I was. I came here and thought, "Wow, I need to be more positive!"

Sometimes, when the students would rather be doing a different activity than what I have planned, I purposely attempt to shift their attention toward recognizing greater possibilities, by using positive phrasing. I'll say, "Well, by doing this *now*, in a little while, you'll have the ability to do *that*" or "If we focus on this for *now*, then it will help us later to do..." Then they begin to focus on, "This is what I need to do *now*, and *then* I can do *that*." It's worked really well with the students.

When I was subbing last year, my brother, who is also a teacher here, was in the room while I was teaching. We were playing a musical game with the children. I said, "Who hasn't had a turn yet?" and he just quietly said, "Who still needs a turn?"

He was coaching me, which is a wonderful thing about the team-teaching here. His coaching helped me to become even more aware of the power of positive phrasing.

Rather than thinking, "I haven't had a turn," instead, they think, "I still need a turn." As silly as that sounds, it creates a different mindset.

Positive phasing is all about focusing attention and language on the things that you want, rather than what you don't want. It's speaking in a way to help set a climate that is filled with possibilities. It really is uplifting to live in this kind of "can-do" environment.

"Play It Their Way"

Bettyann Pitti, Media Specialist
At IDS since 1996

While teaching, I always try to put myself in the students' place before I jump to any conclusions. There's a lot of empathy here in every classroom, and it comes from teachers respecting the students' perspective.

A few years ago, I helped a struggling student after school. I tried to put myself in his place, and felt compassion for how poorly he was feeling. He was having a very hard time, and needed a strong dose of organizational skills.

First, I helped him get organized, so that he had everything written down and could actually check off what he was doing.

Then I looked for his strengths. I noticed that he would write really well when he understood his assignment; and though his handwriting was nearly illegible, he could type.

I learned that he was more of an auditory, rather than a visual learner. One day, when he was overwhelmed, I asked, "Would it help if I read this to you while you typed?" Now for me, that would be horrible. I would not be able to have somebody read to me while I type; so it didn't dawn on me at first that this would be something that could be helpful. But we gave it a try and it worked!

Some people might see that as enabling him, but I was reading from his own written notes as he typed, and that made it so much easier for him to process.

Some think that if the children are listening with their headphones, then they are not really reading. Our philosophy is that it is wise to use multiple resources to meet the learning needs of each student.

Previously, this student had to re-type almost everything he wrote. Now he uses a machine to type his work in class, and he has a lot more self-confidence. This student has become much more organized, his understanding of what he's learning has grown, and he's far more independent than he was in the past. He now does what he needs to do on his own, with a lot less guidance, which is what we always set as the goal.

One of the keys with this student was finding the uniqueness in his learning style, and then tailoring his learning to that style. In so doing, I helped him realize how smart he really is!

P.E. for Everyone!

Coach Jeff Smith and Coach Renee Holden
At IDS since 2000 and 2001

Several intermediate girls were spending so much time talking to each other during team sports one day that the game was losing its momentum.

Pulling them aside, I said, "What can we do to resolve this situation? Why is it that every time we see you, you're standing there talking to each other and taking time from others who are on task?"

The girls replied that they felt they weren't being allowed to take part in the activity. "No one's throwing to us, and no one's passing the ball!" We uncovered their resistance; then we took action by involving them in a decision-making activity.

We decided to make a separate game, and have two games going on simultaneously: one for the people who were really gung-ho and competitive, and the other for people who were just learning how to grasp the game and need a more comfortable pace.

Since it was clear to us what the girls were experiencing, the solution came easily. We remembered going to P.E. and waiting in a line of ten people to kick or hit the ball. It was boring and it was easy to get distracted.

At IDS, our goal is to create an atmosphere where everybody can feel like they're a part of the team. The more opportunities students get to practice a skill or a set of skills, the more likely they will gain confidence while enjoying the game.

Empowerment for Teachers, Parents, and the Community:

Personal and Professional Joy and Satisfaction

A Learning Utopia
What It Feels Like Being Part Of A Think-Tank Community

Jennifer Euliano, Pre-K Teacher
At IDS since 1994

At IDS, we pride ourselves on being knowledgeable about the latest brain research and teacher training. We participate in many courses, which are motivating and energizing!

We believe in developing a life-long learning mentality. We study like a "think tank" – always seeking to find strategies that are developmentally appropriate, to accelerate the learning process.

When I visited IDS as a parent looking at schools for my own children, I remember thinking to myself on my way home, "Wow, this is really a special place, with a balance of positive energy and harmonious calm." For me, it's like a learning utopia for children *and* faculty.

Setting Expectations: Life in a Professional Community

Cynthia Brown, Kindergarten
At IDS since 1999

When I'm at IDS, it's like my home away from home. I feel very comfortable here. There's a very safe feeling, a sense that I can try new approaches, that I can try different strategies, and that I may do so in an atmosphere of professional freedom. People will support me. If my new approach has worked out well, they'll borrow my idea. If it needs tweaking, they'll say, "Let's see how we can make that better."

The way we are trained to teach the students is similar to how the administration facilitates our training. We are all given encouragement to grow.

In some schools, teachers like us are sometimes judged as though they're trying to be better than everybody else. But when you come here, it's what's expected; so there's a greater sense of teamwork.

In our faculty, there is a prevailing sense of, "We need to be the best we can be." We ask ourselves, "How can we help each other?" We teach the children to work cooperatively and tell them that learning together makes them smarter.

I work as a teacher to make learning fun and exciting, so that it feels like every day is a field trip! If you can create that for your students, you can create it for yourself.

Parents Complete the Circle of a Community

Jean Harrison, Kindergarten Teacher
At IDS since 1998

Once you win parents' confidence, everything else is a piece of cake.

I do that by working hard for parents to understand that they can trust me with their child. That means taking the time to talk with them in the morning if they choose to come into the classroom. Some teachers prefer to devote that time just for the students. I create time for parents because that also benefits our students.

I schedule my classroom time so that, in the mornings, the students have several independent team activities for the first half-hour. This way I can also be there for the moms and dads, and even grandparents. Parents appreciate the time and ask advice on a million things relating to their children.

I also constantly e-mail them messages, so that they feel like they are more a part of our day at school. For example, I will share, "So-and-so had a great day," or send digital pictures of their children.

Parents deserve to know I really care about their child. They have to feel their child is "number one." Well, in fact, every child is!

We Are a Family

Roberta Lipschutz, Kindergarten Teacher
At IDS since 1986

The secret to our success is the people that work at IDS. We are here because of our love of children and love of learning. The teachers here are extremely committed to discovering each individual child's learning style.

Even though we've grown from less than 150 students (when I came to IDS) to more than 500, we've been able to retain our style of "hands-on" learning, or learning by doing. Our leadership has always supported us doing this. Our kindergarten and Pre-K team teachers are masters at creating experiences that touch upon all of the Multiple Intelligences and make learning fun!

What touches my heart about IDS is when I walk down the hallway and a class passes me, and they call out my name, reaching out for a hug. I love their love.

A few weeks ago, a parent called me about her child. He was a former kindergartner and now is in our sixth grade. She called me *at home* and said, "Will you please talk to my child? He still listens to you!" I talked to him, and helped him get a broader perspective on things, and gave him tips to help him better understand "parents." We give guidance and support more than just to the children in our class. We are involved with the entire family. The staff at IDS genuinely cares!

Links in the Resource Chain

Kim Fowler, First Grade Teacher
At IDS since 1998

Sometimes, being the best teacher you can be means knowing how to enlist the help of others in various situations. At IDS, there are so many resources available to us, especially our talented faculty. For example, when faced with a challenging situation involving a student, I rely on my team-teacher, Debi. She is my right arm, my partner.

In addition, there are also our Upper-Primary Division (first, second and Multi-Age) meetings each week. These meetings are very valuable. They provide the opportunity to openly explore questions or dilemmas, as well as offer advice or share past experiences to help solve them. We act as resources for one another. Each teacher is rich in knowledge and understanding, dedicated to all of the children in the upper primary grades, in addition to our own students. In order to make sure that we address everyone's ideas and concerns, we apply "group dynamics" skills to facilitate a lively and productive discussion and interaction. These skills are the foundation of our learning community.

Documentation is another great tool. Each child has an academic portfolio, and if necessary, a behavioral portfolio, which we can easily reference alone or during our meetings and conferences. I'll make notes like, "I tried this strategy, and here's how it was resolved."

If I still need assistance in solving the problem, I turn to a teacher who possesses a personal strength or expertise in the specific area. As a total faculty, we work together so often that we know our fellow teachers' academic and professional fortes. Often, I'll discuss the situation with colleagues who are highly adept in understanding different perspectives about students, whether they need more challenges in academics, or whether they are challenged with regard to behavior or learning needs.

If the situation continues to go unresolved, the administration always shows a willingness to assist me and regularly proves to be an excellent resource for handling challenges.

Whenever necessary, I'll bring in the parents, as they're often able to shed light on parts of the child's life I rarely see. By sharing their insights with me about what they observe occurring at home, I'm able to have a broader view of any potentially influential factors.

At IDS, we teachers are constantly looking for options. In our classrooms, our students learn who to turn to for assistance in getting their needs met. And amongst our faculty, so do their teachers.

Three Important Lessons

Jaclyn Kanarish, Primary Multiage, Grades 1 & 2
IDS Resident, 2002-2003

A commitment to "go the extra mile" for every student is a positively contagious tradition at IDS, and makes for a Disney-like experience for both the teachers and the students. Being a resident teacher at IDS means being open-minded, flexible, dedicated to life-long learning, and working hard. During my stay here, I have learned three very important lessons that I will take with me wherever I teach in the future.

First, commit to the children as individuals – not just as a group – by creating every classroom lesson so that it meets the needs of every type of learner. This way, every child can excel.

Second, implement Kagan cooperative structures, so that students can be highly engaged in the learning process. In addition to absorbing more information than in the traditional "desks-books-worksheets" format, students also have many opportunities to develop positive, healthy relationships with their peers.

Third, and most importantly, continue to grow my love of children, of learning and of education. This love motivates me to do whatever it takes to create a learning environment where children feel at ease; because when they do, their "sponge-like" quality increases, and learning becomes a joy for them. Seeing their reactions of excitement as they learn, grow and succeed inspires me to always go above and beyond what is expected.

Teacher Appreciation

Pennie Collins and Jeanne Rivera, Third Grade Teachers
At IDS since 1999 and 1997

What we do here at IDS is purposeful. Even if it's challenging at the moment, you know that the end result is going to be right for the kids. Our leadership is always seeking methods that enable our job to be easier, better and more efficient. Time spent meeting and studying as a faculty leads ultimately to bringing out the best in our students.

Our headmaster, Dr. Swarzman, balances commitment to professional growth with appreciation to build the feeling of community amongst the teachers. For example, in a recent faculty meeting, she had a full agenda planned focusing on curriculum mapping progress across the grade levels. Just before sinking our teeth into the job at hand, she shared a prideful moment congratulating a fellow teacher.

That sparked others to stand, applaud, and appreciate achievements, both professional and personal. It was just inspired by the moment. People passed the microphone giving compliments to individuals and teams for successes, both inside and outside of school. It generated an almost overwhelming feeling of respect and admiration for our peers.

We are appreciated and valued for our interests and accomplishments outside of our professional role, and we are respected as professionals. We're given the freedom to do what's right for kids, within guidelines. The culture of our administration allows for and accepts exploring new options. It feels good to know that we are respected for our opinions.

IDS Residency Program

Heather Robinson, Middle School Science Teacher
and Former Resident; at IDS since 2002

Participating in the one-year residency program at IDS feels like I've gained five years of educational training in school. Now, I feel as though I have *always* been a teacher.

At IDS, a resident spends a full year in a classroom, learning from the same teacher(s) and bonding with the same students. We get to be immersed in the 'real-life' learning environment, with the advantage of having great mentors to model lesson plans, classroom management and other important facets of teaching. As the year progresses, the master teacher(s) step back, and the residents share full responsibility for each class. The insights, tools, and strategies we residents gather while in the IDS classrooms give real-life exposure to teaching, similar to a resident in a hospital gaining a hands-on "doctor" experience.

The teacher-training seminars at IDS are also invaluable, and I have especially appreciated attending Kagan Cooperative Learning workshops, where I have learned specific teaching techniques to meet the individual and team learning needs of each one of my students.

Most of all, I've learned that the teacher-student connection is the most important element in student success and achievement, both academically and socially. Through my residency at IDS, I am steadily increasing my ability and my confidence to create a learning-friendly science classroom environment, where all students have the opportunity to learn to love and absorb science, as well as achieve their personal best!

At IDS, it's not just the students who are learning, but also the teachers. It's really nice to see that the learning community is for everyone.

The Notebook Approach

Fifth Grade Teachers: Linda Wenzel, Director of Studies
Michelle Hill, Division Leader
At IDS since 1996 and 1997

Since teachers are constantly collecting and searching for ideas to improve or create the perfect lesson, the notebook approach is a great organizational tool. Our planning is much more productive since we have implemented this systematic time-saver.

Traditionally, teachers have kept file cabinets filled with file folders containing lesson plans, resources, units or themes. We've found that using three-ring binders to house our lesson plans and resources needed for each lesson is a much more effective strategy for maintaining organization when planning lessons.

Using this system is as easy as collecting a number of two or three-inch notebooks for each subject, topic, and/or theme. We also use index dividers. Plastic sleeves are used to house each lesson plan and the handouts or other relevant resources.

The manner in which notebooks are organized can vary to meet individual needs. Sometimes, it might make sense to organize notebooks by subjects. One might choose to organize notebooks by units or themes. The possibilities are endless. Each teacher can choose to organize the notebooks to best meet his or her needs for planning.

After a lesson is completed, we note changes made during the lesson or changes we wish we had made by writing suggestions on sticky notes and placing them in the notebook. Then they are there to remind us how to do better at implementing the lesson next year.

We regularly look back at what we did, add to it and enhance it. For example, one of our social studies books is on the Civil War. Now we have six notebooks about that period in American history. Using standards and benchmarks, we take the content and create a lesson around it. The notebook has all the resources ready to use for planning and lesson delivery.

We have been creating notebooks for about three years, and we have received additional resources from the developer of the Civil War book. So now, we are taking our original lesson ideas and merging them with the 'new.' We constantly try to "jazz up" our material, to keep our delivery fresh and exciting.

Now we can pull a notebook off our shelf, and we have a great base to start with every single year. Thanks goes to Dr. Mary Giella, whose notebook system has influenced hundreds of teachers through her example during her days as Assistant Superintendent of Pasco County Schools.

Three Keys to Successful Teaming

Fifth Grade Teachers Linda Wenzel, Director of Studies
Michelle Hill, Division Leader
At IDS since 1996 and 1997

What is a team? Depending on the school environment, teaming can take on many forms. In our situation, teaming means four teachers working together to plan, generate ideas, teach, and create a community that stimulates the work force of the future.

Finding the right players who are able to contribute in such a manner is key. We look for people who share our philosophy, and who are interested in life-long learning, in growing professionally and in raising the bar. Since we are often together for more hours of the day with each other than with our own families, it is important we connect; there has to be that sense of belonging.

When beliefs are similar, compromise easily occurs. Teaming requires compromise because lesson delivery might be different in a team situation versus how it might be done if one were self-contained.

Another element to consider when teaming is time. The larger the team, the more time it takes. It's important to choose teammates who are willing to take that time to generate ideas together, develop lessons around those ideas, get excited about sharing, and script out the steps for a lesson so that anyone on the team can teach it.

The beauty of teaming is multi-faceted. Each year, we are able to model the power of cooperation for our students who are also expected to adapt easily to both solo and teamwork. Yet, working with others is both a blessing and a challenge. Since we interact with our peers on a daily basis, the pressure of teaming keeps us on our toes; it allows us the opportunity to continually grow professionally.

Having more heads than one, with different styles and personalities, offers increased opportunity for students to connect with a teacher and/or teachers.

The children enjoy 1) watching us interact, 2) seeing us "huddle" when a new idea comes right in the middle of a lesson, and 3) hearing our laughter with one another as we appreciate how a teammate took the words right out of our mouths. They see us in our most promising light. We model for them how a good team works together.

Top Three Reasons to Teach ...at IDS

Mrs. Linda Boza, Middle School Social Studies
Teacher; at IDS since 1983

Reason #3: Income Opportunities

When I first chose teaching as a career, I overlooked the lack of monetary gain and focused on serving society. It's nice to be idealistic; but as I began to raise my own two children, money became an issue for me. Bluntly, I must say that I am disturbed that our society makes millionaires out of liquor distributors, while teachers must take out loans for their own children to attend college. Nevertheless, I am intensely grateful that IDS provides multiple opportunities for its teachers to conveniently earn extra income. For example, this summer, our school ran thirty-three summer camps. This is a wonderful service to our community, but its top goal is to provide income for our family of diversely talented teachers and coaches.

During the school year, we also offer over fifty after-school clubs. Many parents are always looking for quality activities for their children. For a reasonable fee, our students are given exciting opportunities, parents have a trust-worthy place for their child, and teachers can earn a convenient extra income. It's a win-win!

Reason #2: Creativity is Encouraged

There are pockets of excellence and creativity in every type of school. The difference at IDS is that creativity flourishes *throughout* the school. Teachers at IDS feed off of each other's creativity. If you spread the word that you are working on a particular unit, ideas and supplies start appearing. We are not separated by merit pay or anything that would demise cooperation among the teachers. Cooperation is our theme.

Reason #1: Love

So, I suppose, money and creativity aside, I teach at IDS to be in its community of L-O-V-E. I swell with tears at the two decades of respect, loyalty and support within this school family. I imagine it is the nature of people who choose teaching as a career to be caring, but at IDS it is particularly evident. My colleagues have been there for me through the joys of births and the tears of death. The teachers are my closest support group, but the feeling abounds throughout the school, including administration, office personnel, maintenance team, night security, parents and, most importantly, our loving students. It was IDS students who gave me my first baby shower. It is the culture of the school to love and be loved.

In conclusion, how can this affect you? Once upon a time, I was told that the future of our community would be better off if more students attended IDS. Actually, IDS has wisely capped our size to insure our close feeling of community; but it's true that the future of the world would benefit if more schools were like IDS. Can you nurture a "top three reasons" in your own school community?

That Magic Feeling
High Expectations and Stress-Free Mistakes

Michael LeBlanc, Music Specialist
At IDS since 1998

When we work with the students in music, our expectations are high. The way we set expectations starts with the way we warm up—posture, vocal technique, smiling. All of it is important, and they know from the outset to always give their best. I tell them often that they're great, and that they're going to be great when they perform.

When I make mistakes, I'm pretty open about it. I'll say, "Well, that was just silly." I think it helps them to know that if they make a mistake, it's going to be okay; because I let them know it's simply an opportunity to improve.

Quite often, our headmaster, Joyce, has a very definite idea in her head about what excellence looks and feels like in a particular program, and she'll share it with our music team.

For example, when preparing for school-wide concerts, we always emphasize singing, including vocalization, posture and facial expressions, as would be expected. Now we include choreography, drummers, dancers, public speaking and even sign language! Since some students really enjoy movement, this variety offers an opportunity for them to participate in a way that piques their interests and strengths, too. Making a point to include options that reach every student is well worth the effort.

Taking these "little extra steps" often catapults our lesson or concert from good to great. Planning for these extras often take the most time for our teaching team; and although they can be quite a stretch, we always work to make them reachable. Sometimes the task might be so huge, we'll encourage each other with positive "team-talks," saying, "This is easy. It's what we should be doing anyway. Let's just do it. Let's make sure it's done right, and let's do it now!" Going the extra mile makes all the difference in our ability to help every student experience the joy and satisfaction of a truly successful performance.

The key is to know the feeling we're reaching for, and to create that "WOW!" Now we know that magic feeling. We know how to create magic, because we've been stretched there a few times. The students also love showing their best because they know how much we appreciate those efforts, and the audience appreciates the performance even more. Everyone wins.

We often feel like we're creating miracles with our students; and with everything we have going on, sometimes we need to step back and remember why we're doing it. It's all about kids!

Curriculum Connections in P.E.

Coach Jeff Smith
At IDS since 2000

A YAAG (Year At A Glance) is an organizer-styled system printed on sheets of paper, which help keep me on task and on track as I'm creating lessons throughout the year.

Among our team of P.E. coaches, we share our YAAG's with each other to make sure that we're covering all the necessary knowledge and skills, from Pre-K all the way to eighth grade, so the students are ready when they get to high school.

For example, in sixth grade, the focus is on reviewing and teaching new psychomotor skills, while in seventh grade, the areas of concentration are team sports, cooperation and communication.

We also exchange YAAG's with every teacher in the school. Teachers in all grade levels at IDS frequently exchange YAAGs as a way of making connections across curriculum areas.

I often plan my lessons around a particular teacher's schedule of topics. For example, I teach lacrosse to my students when they are learning about Native American history and culture in social studies. I assigned my sixth grade class a research project where they went online to find games from other countries. Then they had the opportunity to teach it to their classmates. We were able to integrate these games for Multi-Cultural Day. Connections across the curriculum make for rich learning experiences.

PART IV

IDS Press Releases and "IDS Press" Stories

The following collection of IDS press releases and "IDS Press" articles were written by:

Karen Waksman, Managing Editor
and
Mary Beth Erskine, Editor and Writer

The following IDS Press Releases (1999-2003) highlight examples of lessons which provide an additional glimpse into a "brain-friendly" school environment. It is our hope that you will take the ideas and make them your own. We recognize that many of these lessons are already implemented by great teachers found in pockets of excellence throughout the educational world. The uniqueness of our work is an attempt, through study and a "think-tank" approach, to create a total school of excellence.

The Press Releases are arranged as follows:

Primary Programs – Intermediate Programs Middle
School Programs – School-wide Programs
Community Service – Training for Excellence

IDS Press

The following press releases highlight some of the proud moments for our most special gifts – our students. We hope that these articles will give you, the reader, some insight into the caring environment and creative curriculum we work so hard to provide at IDS.

Typically, a call for story ideas for press releases or for our school newsletter produces an abundance of "good stuff" from our faculty and staff, because to them most everything is a special event when it comes to our classrooms. In fact, lessons are created to be special events. Frankly, instruction is expected and designed to be newsworthy in the everyday chronicles of our students' minds as they embrace learning. To accomplish this takes knowledge on how to best connect curriculum and learning.

Therefore, the press releases are filled with memories that are more than just cute activities concocted for fun. Each story is designed as part of a bigger picture that represents how students learn and connect to national and state standards and benchmarks. When we combine brain information with curriculum, then that three-pound, wet, fragile mass called a brain is more likely to be a "user-friendly" ally.

As you read this section, please notice the team-teaching that is woven throughout the stories; faculty teamwork and synergy are some of the most important reasons for student success.

The Evolution of the IDS Warrior

by Dr. Joyce Burick Swarzman, Headmaster
& Pam Ripple, Associate Headmaster

Part I: "Tradition or a Noisy Cat"

"Change is difficult" appears as a common phrase heard in our very fast-paced modern world. Peter Drucker, a writer and business guru on management and leadership, trains his clients and readers to ask, "If you were to begin all over again, what would be absolutely necessary to keep?"

We were given just that opportunity during our 2001 move to the new, beautiful middle school facility. This seemed like a perfect time to begin a new era in IDS history by creating a new, worthy mascot. After all, the connotation of "warrior" seemed to be at odds with our thirty-two year old philosophy statement, charted by our founders, Marilyn Gatlin and Betty Anderson.

When asked to choose a new mascot, many middle schoolers who normally appreciate and thrive on being able to participate in a decision-making process reacted passionately to protect the Warrior as their mascot. When asked why they felt so strongly, many replied, "Because it is our tradition." Some felt "Why change, it's good enough." A minority was excited to have something new. None of us bothered to ask how and why we were the Warriors in the first place.

This wonderful life lesson in group dynamics and organizational change may be best illustrated through a parable found in a newsletter for education published by *Performance Learning Systems* a few years ago:

> *Long ago, a guru and his disciples sat in the temple to pray each evening. The cat of the temple, which was a very noisy cat, disturbed the people who were praying. So the guru commanded that the cat be tied up out of earshot during the evening prayer.*
>
> *Eventually, the guru died, and his disciples continued to tie up the cat during the evening prayer. When in time that cat died, they brought a new cat into the temple so they could continue the tradition of tying it up during evening prayers.*
>
> *A century later, when someone questioned the reason for the practice of cat-tying, the disciples joined together to write a long, sophisticated treatise on its importance in the ritual of the evening's prayer.*

Could it be possible that what we were holding onto was a "Noisy Cat Syndrome?" A search into how the Warrior became the IDS mascot uncovered some extraordinary news. Approximately 18 years ago (five headmasters ago), the Head of School decided the mascot should be the Warriors because he was a devoted graduate of the Chamberlain High School Chiefs. At that time, consensus building or group decision making was overshadowed by the desire to connect IDS with his beloved alma mater. So what were we resisting by changing the mascot... History? Values? Tradition? Or a noisy cat? Was this a "life's lesson" in our midst? What was more important... our philosophy or a questionable tradition with an arbitrary beginning? The story continues...

Part II: Turning Challenges Into Opportunities

At the very foundation of the training that is shared with both faculty and students at IDS lies the power of positive thinking, and the results of positive action. For example, we've all heard: "View the glass as half full, rather than half empty, turn problems into opportunities, lemons into lemonade, mud into mudpies," and so forth.

Perhaps this mascot-naming experience could turn into a perfect opportunity to "walk the talk." Perhaps a tradition with a questionable start could be reframed into a growth opportunity. A search through a thesaurus and through dictionaries led to some interesting interpretations of "warrior." Perhaps the IDS Warrior could now remain with a new twist – one that represents the best in all of us, one that sets high expectations and goals that bring pride to one's "heart and soul."

Thus, the IDS Warrior for the twenty-first century was born to stand on its own and to lead us proudly into the future.

The IDS Warrior for the 21st Century

Characteristics:

Strong, brave, courageous, heroic, valiant.

Protector of:

Kindness, caring, justice, human potential, the rights of all, decency, the highest values of peace, harmony, compassion and cooperation.

Weapons of Service:

WORDS that are uplifting and encouraging.

ACTIONS that demonstrate respect and dignity for self and others.

A HEART that beats courageously with warmth and strength, kindness and justice, self-confidence and humility.

PRIMARY PROGRAMS

"Centifest" Festivities Add Up To A Mathematical Celebration

At IDS, the first Friday in February was more than just the end of another week in school for our Pre-K through second graders. It was a day for celebrating math – and the 100th day of being in school – with a variety of hands-on, math-related activities.

While teachers and students celebrate student success and the learning experience daily at IDS, the 100th day of school is cause for special festivities. Pre-K, kindergarten, first and second grade students and teachers call it the annual "Centifest."

"Centifest has become an IDS tradition in the primary grades," said first grade teacher and Upper Primary Division Leader Debi Brockmeyer. "We have an annual Science Fair to celebrate science and a yearly Young Author's Day to celebrate writing. Centifest is our way to celebrate math."

During Centifest, students circulated in small, multi-grade teams among the primary classrooms taking part in activities that involved multiple intelligences and focused on the number 100. They colored, cut and painted to create 100-day badges and ladybugs, as well as 100 valentines for patients at a local veterans hospital. A visual/spatial activity involved manipulating 100 plastic cubes to create a design on graph paper. They also participated in "centi-aerobics," physical activities such as throwing a ball or Frisbee to reinforce the concept of 100 centimeters.

Centifest festivities were the culmination of numerous projects based on 100, many of which had been taking place in classrooms since the beginning of school. First graders, for example, had a goal of reading 100 books. Several classes kept track of "Acts of Kindness" with 100 as their target. All students brought in collections of 100 items, which they sorted, counted and compared to integrate a variety of mathematical skills. Teachers also incorporated literature into their focus on 100. Pre-K students, for example, combined collections of 100 edible items to create a class pie after reading Audrey Woods' popular *Sweet Dream Pie*.

"For young students, the number 100 is a really important concept," said Pre-K teacher Jessica Schew. "Centifest makes the number real to them with a variety of hands-on learning activities."

From the Human Body to Sign Language: Primary Students Leap into Learning

Do you know what part of the body cleans your blood? The Pre-K and kindergarten classes at IDS do – they began the school year with an exciting thematic unit on the human body. One of the activities related to this unit involved body tracing. Each child's body was traced on extra long sheets of butcher paper, and the students decorated their tracings to resemble themselves. Then, as they learned about the various organs in the body, they added these parts to their "paper bodies."

Students experienced many hands-on experiments throughout this unit such as a pumping station that demonstrated the workings of the heart. They also studied actual animal organs, including chicken and calf livers, pig brains, a chicken heart, and cow intestines. To conclude their investigations into the body, the classes studied the five senses and nutrition, wrapping up with a field trip to Publix grocery store.

Coming up for Pre-K and kindergarten will be an in-depth study of their class mascots. One class will learn about the life cycle and hatching of chicks. All Pre-K and kindergarten classes weighed, measured and carved (with parent help) pumpkins for Halloween, and will participate in the annual Living Thanksgiving to learn about the life of a Pilgrim.

Just in time for the November election, the first grade "Cool Cats" studied the "Good Ol' U.S.A." Students concluded this unit with their first project reports during which they had the opportunity to teach their classmates about a state of their choice.

Multi-age class students learned about making good choices for their bodies involving nutrition and exercise during their first trimester unit of study, "Challenges, Choices and Solutions."

All first and second grade classes have been coming together twice a week for Multi-Age Academic Enrichment time. Classes are "mixed up" during this period so students can experience different content areas with different teachers and students, and every four weeks students switch to a new subject area. These areas include: Reader's Theatre, Cooking Around the World, Inventions, Science Investigations, Sign Language and Stretching Your Mind. According to the teachers, Multi-Age time has not only been enhancing the curriculum, but has been building a community of caring and enthusiastic learners – who are having fun!

The "Top Bananas" in Mrs. Ehrlich's and Mrs. Harrison's classes are enthusiastic learners, as well. They began the first trimester by exploring many techniques and strategies that will empower them to become independent, creative and critical thinkers.

In reading, Top Bananas have been applying skimming and scanning highlighting techniques to help them locate information. In language arts, they have been using formula writing and creative themes to refine their paragraph writing, including creating Halloween rebus stories. "Top Banana Spelling Techniques" have been giving them practice with phonetic patterns, visual configuration, and suffixes – and they have even been "finger writing" in shaving cream to reinforce spelling words!

Daily Mad Minute math solo tests, science games, Venn diagrams, and cartography have also been popular with the Top Bananas. They began mapping by sketching Lake Lipsey and illustrating the playground area, and then created their own table map, adding a compass rose, coordinates, symbols and map keys.

Primary division students at IDS have certainly taken a giant "leap into learning" during this year's first trimester!

Bringing the Study of Outer Space Down to Earth

The imaginations of the youngest IDS students took flight and soared straight into space earlier this school year. During the first trimester, Pre-K and kindergarten students studied the solar system and the universe in many creative and thought-provoking ways, giving their minds the opportunity to contemplate the cosmos, while their feet remained firmly planted on the ground.

Providing the perfect combination of mystery, imagination and science to keep young minds engaged, this thematic unit of study was an exciting one for students, according to the Pre-K and kindergarten teaching team. "At this age, the children are very interested in the study of space," says division leader and Pre-K teacher Karen Jankowski. "They've heard a little bit about it, and they're so eager to know more."

"Some children really know a lot of information about certain objects in space," says kindergarten teacher Jean Harrison. "This unit allows us to tap into their intelligence in this area. We can offer them the opportunity to really stretch and learn how certain things in outer space affect the Earth where they live."

Designed to help students understand the interaction and organization of the solar system and the universe and how space affects life on earth, the unit culminated in a field trip to the Museum of Science and Industry's planetarium and Discovery Room to reinforce the vastness of the universe and the Earth's place in it.

"The students have fun studying space because they're learning about things that are relevant to them," says kindergarten teacher Cindy Fontana. "They look up at the sky and they can see the sun, the moon, and the stars. It's real to them. They come to realize that they're part of a huge universe."

Walking through the Pre-K and kindergarten classrooms during these weeks revealed a wide range of hands-on activities and special areas of study. For example, after learning about the constellations and how people long ago told stories about the stars, students drew their own constellations, adding dinosaurs, giraffes and alien birds to the night sky. Bright tissue paper suns hanging from the ceilings and charts listing "moon facts" were visual reminders of discussions, answering questions about the sun, the moon, and the planets, relating to rotation and revolution."

Throughout the study of space, there were numerous opportunities for young students to do what they do best – use their imaginations – to become astronauts flying through space or strap thick sponges to their feet and walk across the surface of the moon. Each Pre-K and kindergarten class worked cooperatively to construct its own rocket ship or space shuttle from large boxes, adding aluminum foil, stickers, lights, windows and other personal touches; and those rocket ships and shuttles became the center of many adventures and exciting space simulations.

"The spaceship was an area where we could constantly hear the children's learning being applied," says Pre-K teacher Michelle Robson. "The concepts being introduced became part of their creative play, just as planned."

In Mrs. Jankowski's class, students defined a space mission, decided what they would need for their mission, and then mapped it out. Many classes launched their own film canister rockets from paper plate launch pads using Alka-Seltzer as fuel. Jennifer Euliano's Pre-K students learned about the earth moving through space by studying shadows. "The hands-on, physical lessons help them internalize concepts," she says. "It helps them make connections between what they're actually doing and the study of space."

The wide range of hands-on activities "addressed multiple intelligences and interest levels," says kindergarten teacher Roberta Lipschutz. "They experienced 'real life' exploration of science and nature, learning that there is a world beyond them – and it extends beyond the solar system."

First Graders Participate in "Pioneer Olympics"

What do you get when you combine the study of life as a pioneer with lessons in measurement during an Olympic year? If you're a first grader at IDS, you get the opportunity to participate in the school's inaugural "Pioneer Olympics."

According to the first grade teaching team of Kim Fowler and Debi Brockmeyer, who introduced the unusual concept to their students, the events that comprised this type of Olympics were variations on traditional Olympic favorites with every measuring activity based on a pioneer theme.

For example, instead of the discus throw, there was the "Cow Chip Throw," with paper plates substituting for the real thing. During the "Hay Stack Javelin Throw," yellow pipe cleaners were used as hay. Cotton balls were pint-size tumbleweeds for the "Tumbleweed Toss," and the "Cow Milking" competition had students measuring how much water they could squeeze out of a sponge.

Mrs. Fowler and Ms. Brockmeyer applied the idea of a Pioneer Olympics to the first grade curriculum as an innovative, hands-on way to reinforce mathematical skills in standard and non-standard forms of measurement and integrate social studies lessons about pioneers.

"Integrating lessons helps a child make connections and see that everything goes together in the real world," says Ms. Brockmeyer.

"This experience gave meaning as to why we were doing measurement," said Mrs. Fowler. "Students got to see that it's not just something in a book, but that we do it all the time."

From Depth to Diameter: Independent Day School Second Graders Measure Pond

For second graders at IDS, Pond Measuring Day has become a much-anticipated tradition. It's the day these young scientists strap on life jackets, and with paddles in hand, march proudly down to the school's pond. There, they board canoes and with parents as their guides, they measure the pond -- from temperature, to depth, to diameter -- in every direction.

For second grade teachers Fran Ehrlich and Catherine Harrison, Pond Measuring Day is the culmination of weeks of study in a variety of areas with the total integration of skills in science, math, social studies, language arts and reading. "Pond Measuring Day is a unique lesson that typifies the IDS approach to learning that takes place every day, in every classroom," said Ehrlich.

According to Ehrlich, Pond Measuring Day was designed to teach mathematical concepts such as inches, feet, yards, volume, depth, temperature, circumference and diameter – and their practical uses.

"It's a hands-on way to make concrete connections between learning and everyday life," said Harrison. "The students make their own tools for measuring depth and temperature. They use boat line sinkers to use as depth finders and attach strings to thermometers. They also learn how to use the compass to understand directionality, so they can measure the entire pond."

To prepare for the big day, students practiced measuring on land. They found the diameter of everything from playground equipment tunnels and bottle caps, to a small plastic pool brought into the classroom to simulate the real pond. According to the teachers, skills from every discipline of the second grade curriculum were reinforced.

In Social Studies, for example, students studied the Compass Rose and mapping. In math, they learned how to graph and problem solve, read and compare temperatures, measure with standard and non-standard tools, and measure with metrics and Standard English forms.

Science lessons focused on the scientific method of discovery. Students formulated and tested their hypotheses, predicting how deep they thought the pond was in each area – then verified their guesses with actual measurements. They utilized balancing principles, invented measuring tools, and identified flora and fauna in the IDS environment. Language arts and reading lessons centered on following directions, journal writing, letter writing and formula writing and reading.

In addition to measuring the pond, students drew maps, sketched the pond, participated in nature scavenger hunts, kept journals of the day's activities and collected any trash around the pond area. While every student enjoyed the day, each had a favorite activity. Some enjoyed making the measuring tools best. Others liked taking turns and working as a team on both water and land activities.

"I really liked learning how to record all the depths and temperatures," commented one student. "I also liked throwing in the thermometer. We had to do that carefully, so we wouldn't shake the canoe."

"I liked measuring the diameter," another student shared, "because someone on the land had to hold the string while we went across the pond in the canoe."

"For me, the best part was the nature scavenger hunt, because I found a lot of new things I didn't know were there," said a third student.

"Pond Measuring Day is a prime example of the interconnectedness of learning," said Ehrlich, "so we involve teachers of other content areas, as well." While they were learning to measure in math class, for example, the students were also learning canoe safety in their physical education class. Parents also got involved, as volunteer canoe guides who helped the students row out into the pond to take the measurements they needed.

Ehrlich said, "Our students were thrilled to learn that they could measure the pond's diameter and then use a formula to determine the circumference." Teachers, students and their parents agree that Pond Measuring Day was a very entertaining way to do math.

Pond Day also teaches students about community, teamwork, leadership and group dynamics. By teaming up, the work is distributed, and so is the weight of the canoe when they carry it to the water! They learn about leadership, because each child has a job responsibility.

"I like Pond Day so much because it teaches the students so many important skills, both in their academic and social lives. At IDS, the opportunities to enjoy a rich, stimulating and fun learning environment are seemingly endless! These relevant opportunities are peak experiences for both myself and my students!" Ehrlich said.

MAE Disguises Learning As Volcanoes, Cooking and Fun!

In the second grade classrooms, Fran Ehrlich's students chop apples, measure corn oil, and mix batter for apple cake. Catherine Harrison's students witness the flow of "molten rock," as vinegar and baking soda erupt inside their tabletop volcano.

First grade teacher Kim Fowler passes out playing cards to the students in her class who then discuss the cards' various attributes and create Venn diagram models. Next door, Debi Brockmeyer's students sing a song about world peace.

In the Multi-Age classrooms, Jennifer Jones' students mix "mystery" ingredients together as they conduct an experiment about evaporation. Michelle Carlo shares a blueprint with her class for a scale model of the Eiffel Tower that they will construct from colorful straws and connectors.

For first, second, and Multi-Age students at IDS, it's one of the many highlights of the week – MAE time. Technically, MAE stands for Multi-Age Academic Enrichment, but for these students, learning stands for fun!

Initiated by the first, second and Multi-Age teaching team last year, MAE is a special period twice a week when students from each class are grouped into six teams to experience new subject areas with different teachers and students. They change to a different topic and teacher every four weeks.

The teachers all agree that MAE enhances the upper primary division curriculum taking it beyond core subjects.

INTERMEDIATE PROGRAMS

Teaching to the Heart

An acrobat learning to leap from one trapeze to the next knows that if he throws his heart over the bar first, his body will follow. Likewise, the teachers at IDS believe that if you teach to a child's heart, everything else can fall into place.

"Candy grams" are a unique opportunity for students to learn about operating a business. Several times a year (in celebration of Halloween, winter holidays, and Valentines Day), third graders design, test market, and manufacture greeting cards. They advertise throughout the school, take orders and fill them. Students mail their cards via the IDS mail system, the Peacock Post. The third graders then collect the cards, attach a piece of candy to each one, sort them, cancel the stamps, and make the deliveries.

For IDS third graders, the candy gram business began as a hands-on study of the basics of economics. When it was all over, however, the most valuable lesson these students learned had less to do with math, marketing and money than it did with matters of the heart.

Usually the profits from the candy gram business are used to offset the cost of a class field trip to St. Augustine. According to the third grade teaching team of Pennie Collins, Judy Sobel and Jeanne Rivera, students wanted to do something with the profits from the December sales that would put their class motto, "Care, Share, Help" into action.

After processing nearly 3,000 candy grams before winter break, the students donated their proceeds to a children's home in Tampa.

"These children don't have what we have," said one third grader. "So it made me feel really good to donate the money to them."

Earlier in the year, the class took their "Care, Share, Help" motto on the road when they visited a Carrollwood nursing home to sing for the residents on Halloween. After performing, the students mingled with the elderly patients, sharing handshakes and smiles with a grateful audience.

"The visit to the nursing home was a powerful experience for the children," said Collins. According to Rivera, "it showed them that they have the ability to bring a smile to someone's face with just a handshake or a song."

"Academics are important," said Sobel. "We feel compassion and caring must also be taught, because these are the things they will always carry with them. That's why we teach to the mind, and also to the heart."

Literature Circles

In fourth grade, students began the first trimester by establishing Literature Circles, which work much like a book club for adults. First, students participated in a teacher-led "book look," where teachers shared an overview of the book's plot and described its genre. Next, each fourth grader took a "book walk," perusing each book to decide on his or her top three reading choices. Mrs. Hutchinson, Mrs. Gancedo and Ms. Rudolph then collaborated to place each student in a Literature Circle – and with much success. The teachers said students "beamed" when their book and literature circle assignments were announced.

Now in full swing, Literature Circles meet to set reading goals and discuss individual jobs. Jobs rotate with each discussion meeting and include discussion director, "vocabulary enricher" and illustrator. The entire fourth grade community has been enjoying this opportunity to appreciate and study literature on a mature, in-depth level.

Fifth Graders Bring
the Civil War to Life

When IDS fifth graders headed back to school for their class sleep-over, they brought some unusual supplies with them – sheets and ropes to make pup tents, old socks to darn, mess kits and canteens of water. These were just a few of the things they needed, as they were transformed into the Fifth Grade Regiment located at Camp Lipsey during the Civil War.

Conceived by the fifth grade teaching team led by Division Leader Michelle Hill and Director of Studies Linda Wenzel, the Civil War simulation began with a dinner of hardtack and stew that students had prepared themselves. As an opportunity to reinforce mathematical concepts, students planned their dinner by purchasing their ingredients and preparing the food during the day before.

During dinner, they watched a Civil War reenactment performer demonstrate how the drums commanded the troops during battle. Then, students dressed in authentic clothing of Union and Confederate soldiers to simulate a battle behind enemy lines. Their "scaled down" reenactment was complete with "injured" soldiers, who were brought to medical stations, where their wounds were attended to by "nurses," also outfitted in clothing of that period.

During the evening, the "soldiers" wrote letters home using both quills and the vocabulary specific to the time. The musical portion of the evening included a Virginia Reel, during which they danced and participated in a sing-along. "Mail call" included surprise packages from home, filled with typical items a soldier would have received.

Students set up camp constructing mock pup tents. In the morning, they made butter and cooked breakfast outside. The simulation ended with a guest presentation of an authentic camp and the construction of lanterns similar to those of the period.

"We wanted to create a powerful memory for students through a meaningful learning experience that simulated the reality of the Civil War period," said Mrs. Wenzel.

"In a traditional classroom, you read the chapter, answer the questions, and move on. We believe that the more students can experience the Civil War, the more they will remember its life lessons."

Creating unique learning experiences – and a unique learning environment – is what IDS is all about.

"A Whole Lot of Reading Goin' On"

Sprawled out on the floor and under tables, propped up on pillows with favorite snacks close at hand, IDS fourth graders were so quiet you could hear the classroom computers humming. Perhaps that's because it was April 11th, the day of the fourth grade Read-A-Thon, and they had 180 minutes to do something they love – read!

Similar to a Walk-A-Thon, the students had collected pledges for each minute they would read, and after the Read-A-Thon, collected their pledges. The money raised was applied to the cost of a special year-end field trip to Walt Disney World's Magic Kingdom. There, students took part in an educational program called "The American Story."

"The program at Disney focused on our entire year's social studies curriculum with lots of hands-on activities," says teacher Lisa Hutchinson, who is part of the fourth grade team with Vickii Ausburn and Christine Pringle.

"We planned the Read-A-Thon because we wanted to give students greater ownership by providing a way for them to contribute to the cost of the trip," says Mrs. Gancedo.

"Since the students at IDS are very committed to reading, what better way to encourage them to read than to incorporate reading into one of our fundraisers?" adds Miss Rudolph.

"The Read-A-Thon was a good idea," said another student. "It gave us a chance to earn money for the trip and also to be responsible."

Economics Program Empowers Third Graders

For all the excitement, it could easily have been a Sotheby's auction house in London or New York with a Monet original or a Barry Bonds record-breaking home run baseball up for bid.

The locale, however, was the third grade classroom of IDS, where students wiggled in their chairs, waving makeshift paddles during vigorous bidding. Used candlesticks, slightly worn paperbacks, costume jewelry, and fragrant soaps were some of the popular items they were eager to purchase – each a treasure in its own right because it would become a memorable holiday gift for a special family member.

While the money wasn't real, the lessons in economics, mathematics, and individual responsibility were. Third grade teachers Pennie Collins, Jeanne Rivera and Judy

Sobel designed the auction to culminate students' efforts in earning classroom currency called "moola" throughout the first trimester.

"Our economics program is a real life simulation of earning, saving, and spending income," said Sobel. "It is a motivational system that rewards students for academic excellence and for being responsible third grade citizens."

Students received compensation each Friday for completed homework, academic participation, classroom jobs, responsible behavior and quality work.

As an introduction to the difference between a cash and a cashless society, sometimes students were paid by check, and other times with moola "cash." They recorded their monetary rewards in a check register, and returned it to the class bank. On the day of the auction, every student's checkbook balance was posted. Parents acted as auctioneers, accountants, and gift wrappers and assisted students with the purchase of the new and used items collected within the third grade community during previous weeks.

"Our goal with this program is to incorporate math and economic standards into daily instruction, while familiarizing students with real world functions, such as keeping an accurate balance in a checkbook, and knowing how to fill in a check," said Rivera. "We also want to motivate students to be responsible producers and consumers, and encourage a positive attitude toward class work."

The auction is one of two special occasions where the students have an opportunity to spend their moola. The other is a Bizarre Bazaar, held toward the year's end. At the Bazaar, the children run their own businesses and "sell" their products and services to all students from Pre-K through fifth grade, in exchange for moola, which other teachers give out to their students as an incentive just before the event.

"This approach to economics really empowers students and gives them the opportunity to be independent," said Collins. "They are responsible for earning moola by doing their jobs at school and contributing to the class. They learn to work towards a goal by saving, so they can eventually spend their moola on things they really want for their family."

It is a real life experience that turns used games and trinkets into priceless gifts, and student success into an invaluable lesson.

Multi-Age Science:
A Science in Itself
A Parent's Perspective

The IDS curriculum establishes a strong science foundation for students, while building connections to the basic skills of reading, writing and mathematics. In this article, a parent shares her discovery of cutting-edge learning at its best.

How can you teach science to third, fourth and fifth graders together? Do they all learn the same thing? How many teachers do they have?

You may have had similar concerns. I know I did. I'm a second-year IDS parent of a fourth grader. I, like some of you, perhaps, was a bit confused about this "Multi-Age" thing. So I set out to answer these questions and ask a few of my own. Here's what I found out.

The hands-on philosophy which makes IDS unique is alive and well in the Multi-Age science curriculum in the Intermediate Division (grades 3, 4 and 5). Amidst a superb outdoor environment, students in different grades mutually benefit from each other's skills, while building a sense of community and belonging.

Implemented in 1998, the intermediate science program is an innovative Multi-Age program based on a three-year cycle, whereby third, fourth and fifth graders rotate through four nine-week cycles, learning the same thing, at the same time, in the same class. The program focuses on the application of the scientific method and science processing skills. Students participate in a project / experiment-based / discovery-learning model and are involved in experiences designed to engage their interests, to stimulate curiosity and to develop higher-level thinking skills.

Classwork and tests are graded on an age-appropriate basis. For example, fifth graders are expected to go into more detail than third graders, use better sentence structure and correct spelling.

The four main topics of study are Life, Earth, Physical and Discovery. Each year, these four topics are then broken down into more specific areas of study. These can range from the simple study of weather, under the Earth Science umbrella, to the more complex, like building a model in Discovery science.

Another advantage to Multi-Age science is that teacher experts in each of the four sciences teach the students. The teachers team up in two's or three's selecting one of the four areas that they will teach in depth over the three-year cycle. This not only introduces students to some of their future teachers, but they also learn different teaching styles and personalities.

In a nutshell, by pairing the three age groups, Multi-Age science capitalizes on the uninhibited sense of discovery of the younger child. Exposing him or her to advanced concepts also builds academic skills, while fostering leadership in older students. By the end of the third cycle, students will have thoroughly covered 12 different science subjects, preparing them for middle school programs that will continue to develop their skills as scientists, problem-solvers, designers and engineers.

MIDDLE SCHOOL PROGRAMS

Annual Poetry Coffeehouse

It was a night for wearing black turtleneck sweaters and dark shades – a night for snapping your fingers and listening to poetry. IDS middle school students returned to the days of bongos and beatniks when they hosted the Second Annual Poetry Coffeehouse in Corbett Hall.

Under the direction of English teachers Michael Vokoun and Linda Boza, sixth, seventh and eighth graders performed a wide variety of poetry selections – from Langston Hughes and Robert Frost to Shel Silverstein and Jack Prelutsky – in an intimate, "coffeehouse" setting complete with coffee, sweets and refreshments.

According to Mr. Vokoun, while the purpose of the evening was "to ignite a love of poetry," it also provided students with an opportunity to enhance their speaking skills, while hearing as many different types of poetry as possible.

Each student had delved into his/her own poem to find the speaker, the setting, the meter and the emotions of his/her piece, and dressed appropriately to the needs of the poem. Because some poems used more than one voice, some students performed together. Four sixth grade students from Mr. Bronson's drama class, for example, took on a metrically challenging piece called *Phillip Glass.*

"The students were so excited about doing this," he explains. "Some performed solo and others in groups – some even with props and costumes. One pair of students even had their grandmothers sew a snake costume for them, just for the evening's festivities." That costume is now proudly displayed on Mr. Vokoun's classroom wall.

Sixth Graders Learn Lessons for Living During Annual "People Fair"

While visitors flocked to the Florida State Fair in February, students at IDS hosted a fair of their own. Instead of cotton candy and corn dogs, however, these students served healthy portions of history.

The third annual IDS People Fair gave sixth graders the opportunity to select a person who they believed had a positive impact on the world and in whom they had a particular interest. Selections ran the gamut from historical to contemporary, from sports figures and politicians to scientists and musicians.

Students' hard work culminated in the two-day fair, during which they dressed in costume and portrayed their historical person for other IDS students, parents and guests.

Middle school teacher Linda Boza says participating in the fair enabled students to develop a variety of skills related to English and Social Studies; however, there were other lessons they learned that would help prepare them not only for high school, but also for life. These lessons included determination, kindness, perseverance, and compassion.

"The purpose of this project was to provide a meaningful and interesting reason to do research, to write and to deliver a speech," said Boza. "We also wanted students to prove how their person was a role model or an inspiration. In many cases, that meant weaving through the good and the bad of someone's life to see how they overcame difficulties to become successful."

Students prepared letters and journals written from their person's point-of-view and timelines that illustrated their person's accomplishments. In addition, they collected "artifacts" related to their historical figure and composed original monologues.

For one student, who portrayed Walt Disney, the People Fair was more than a research project. She says, "It was a chance to learn about other people's dreams."

Making Science "Eggs-citing" "Eggs-periments", Engineering, and Nature

Middle school students dropped raw eggs from the top of Raymond James Stadium again this year as part of an annual IDS event that always produces highly innovative ideas and interesting concepts. "The object of the activity is to package an egg according to certain specifications, so that it will not break when dropped from a height," says science teacher Gery Morey. The project accompanies the student's units on science and technology and on force and motion.

A Delicate "Eggs-periment"

Sixth graders use packaging materials and parachutes to protect one raw egg. For seventh graders, the object is to design a structure to hold one raw egg inside, and build a structure or shape on the outside of the container to slow the rate of descent. For eighth graders, the rules are the same as for seventh grade students – except that *two* raw eggs are used!

The students come up with some extremely clever and innovative concepts. "One student has used the same design each year, because it was so successful and so simple – just a paper plate and a paper cone under it to hold the egg," Mrs. Morey said.

One seventh grader used a paper plate with weights glued to the underside and her egg rubber-banded to the top. The plate floated to the ground and was safe. Another student used a straw cage to hold his egg. The structure of crossed straws was enough to break the fall of the container and his egg survived. A sixth grade student built his cage out of craft sticks and put the egg inside. "The container fell and broke apart on impact, but his egg rolled out of the cage in perfect condition!" Mrs. Morey said.

Engineering Marvels

Rube Goldberg created drawings of absurdly complex devices for performing simple tasks. Hence, the term, "Rube Goldberg" denotes a roundabout means of doing something simple. While studying a unit on force and motion, eighth grade students worked in teams to design and build their own Rube Goldberg machines, a task that tied in acceleration and velocity. Each machine did a task in at least three steps when a metal ball was dropped into it. Some examples of the tasks included popping a balloon and allowing a car to run down a track.

"This was a great way to learn about both science and teamwork," says Mrs. Morey.

Getting Back to Nature

As part of their unit on Ecology, seventh graders traveled to Emerson Park on the mouth of the Manatee River to plant native grasses in a wetland. They worked with the Department of Environmental Protection to restore an estuary wetland to its natural state.

"The students felt good about the community service aspect of this project and knowing that they had helped restore our environment," said Mrs. Morey

Whether it's designing egg drop containers or Rube Goldberg machines to learn about force and motion, or putting on old clothes and beach shoes to work in a wetland, the science objective is the same. According to Mrs. Morey, "The goal in middle school is cooperative work through hands-on experiences and Kagan structures to allow students to 'own' the projects that they do in class."

IDS 7th Graders Explore Steinbeck Classic in Novel Way
Marketing Skills and Literature Highlight Classroom Instruction

Students at IDS played the part of movie producer after studying John Steinbeck's *Of Mice and Men*. It's another example of how IDS incorporates different learning styles into everyday classroom instruction.

Drawing upon their creative and artistic skills, each student pitched to a fellow classmate the story's concept and characters, complete with casting choices and a poster created to promote the movie, *Of Mice and Men*. Prior to class presentations, students read the novel in class with an audio version playing at the same time. At certain points, the class stopped to discuss the actions and motivations of the book's characters and the choices that were made.

Michael Vokoun, who team-teaches with Lynne Grigelevich, notes, "Typically, this book is used in high school English classes. I believe that seventh grade students need the opportunity to be exposed to great literature and to be able to offer their take on the story."

To ensure a deeper understanding of the story, students created journals that described each main character, including his or her personality. Descriptions were based on two or more direct quotes, paraphrased material, and general understandings of the characters.

Vokoun stated, "It's 2003, and the book was written in 1937. What can the students glean from a story that is considered a classic? What themes are still issues in today's world and in the student's daily lives?"

When surveyed about the book's ideas and messages, one student said, "It teaches about real life, how to treat others." Another commented that it shows "all things happen for a reason."

Grigelevich added, "I'm so proud of all of the students and how they each brought their own personality and understandings to the assignment!"

Pi Day Comes to IDS

On Tuesday, March 14th, Middle School students at IDS celebrated, of all things, a number, but not just any number. They celebrated the number pi. Why does Pi Day fall on March 14th? Not only is pi approximately equal to 3.14, but 3-14 also happens to be the birthday of a relatively famous mathematician-scientist by the name of Albert Einstein.

"Our students understand the mathematical concept of pi being an irrational, never-repeating number," said math teacher Tom Bronson. "What we want to do is breathe some fun into math, so they feel totally comfortable with it."

Under the direction of Bronson and his teaching partner Thelma Rosenberg, IDS students were given the choice of five different activities in which to participate. They wrote poems using the digits of pi, made necklaces using colored beads to represent the different digits of pi, and also drew works of art using pi both as a symbol and a number.

A play-on-words happened at the last couple of booths. While students were celebrating the number pi, they were also able to enjoy some tasty slices of pie. Students could have brought their own slice or even competed in a pie eating contest (the most amount of slices swallowed on one minute).

"We have a lot of fun, but the highlight of the day is always the pie-throwing contest," said Bronson. "I guess there's something about throwing a whipped cream pie at your math teacher that really drives home the significance of the number pi." Einstein would be proud.

'History Alive'
Taps into Multiple Intelligences

From ancient Greece to the Battle of Antietem. From the Boston Tea Party to China. Every day, middle school students in Barbara Grady and Linda Boza's classes go beyond textbooks and lectures, as they study world and American history and geography. They learn history by experiencing it with all their senses and emotions, as well as their minds.

Listening to music. Singing. Acting out skits. Producing period newspapers. Writing in historical diaries. Interpreting visuals. Sampling foods from around the world. Middle school teachers at IDS make history come alive so students can encounter it firsthand. It could be creating papier-mâché globes in Mrs. Boza's class or analyzing the Boston Massacre by acting it out in Mrs. Grady's class. History lessons become dynamic, participative experiences implemented in the classroom using the typical IDS approach that puts Kagan and other cooperative learning techniques into action.

"We make sure that there's always something to do so that history is not solely listening to lectures and taking notes," says Mrs. Grady.

For example, when her eighth graders were studying Thomas Payne's *Common Sense*, Mrs. Grady formed small groups of students and gave each group a passage to interpret. When they were finished, each group created a skit to share their understanding of these excerpts. Mrs. Boza involves the entire sixth grade in a model United Nations conference that is conducted each year by the YMCA. And when the class studies China, she takes them on a field trip to the outdoor museum in Orlando, "Splendid

China," where students act as tour guides explaining Chinese history and culture.

To help bring history to life and to engage diverse learners, Mrs. Grady and Mrs. Boza use cutting edge educational materials provided by the Teachers' Curriculum Institute called *History Alive!* – a program used daily by more than 30,000 teachers across the country in elementary, middle and high school social studies lessons.

"The best part about *History Alive!* is that it helps us in our effort to address all multiple intelligences," says Mrs. Grady.

"*History Alive!* materials are very student-discovery oriented," says Mrs. Boza. "We use them to help 'show' students history, rather than 'tell' them about it."

For example, the interactive slide lectures enable sixth graders to take a boat trip up the Nile River to see ancient monuments, before creating a travel brochure about the sites they saw and Pharaohs who created them. Placards and slides also allow eighth graders to visualize life in colonial America, so they can discover historical concepts, such as the events that contributed to growing tensions between the columnists and the British. Small groups analyze an image and then assessments are shared with the entire class.

Both Mrs. Boza and Mrs. Grady incorporate experiential exercises into their class lessons. Recreating historical situations such as the turn-of-the-century assembly line or taxation without representation gives students the opportunity to actually feel the emotions of the people of the time.

"When we study the feudal system, we assign students roles and make trades with food and land cards," explains Mrs. Boza. "We also tie the students' shoelaces to their desks to show how the serfs were tied to the land. This really helps them understand the power of the lords and the struggles of the serfs."

Music is another powerful way in which students feel the drama of history. Sometimes it's by learning and singing all the verses to "Yankee Doodle" or by creating and performing an African "call and response" song. "When we were studying about the Nez Perce Indians' retreat from the U.S. Calvary, I played the song, "Heart of the Appaloosa" for them, instead of just lecturing about it," says Mrs. Grady, "and the lyrics really touched their emotions more than my words ever could."

According to Mrs. Boza and Mrs. Grady, the bottom line is that all students can be successful when it comes to learning history.

Source: www.teachtci.com

SCHOOL-WIDE PROGRAMS

Cooperation "Reigns Supreme" at IDS Field Day

Field Day at IDS was a time for fun and games, Popsicles and popcorn. Yet, more important than any of the activities offered, was the opportunity the afternoon provided students to strengthen cooperative skills, as older students acted as both coaches and cheerleaders for their younger counterparts.

To enhance teamwork and community spirit, middle school students in grades six, seven and eight, and fifth graders were paired with primary students in Pre-Kindergarten, kindergarten, first and second grades. Intermediate students in grades three and four also teamed up to support and encourage each other, as they participated in the wide variety of events, ranging from balloon volleyball and obstacle courses to parachute games and rope climbing.

"Field Day provided a fun, safe day where every success was recognized and applauded, and where cooperation reigned supreme," says Kathy Folen, physical education teacher.

According to Coach Kathy Folen, Field Day at IDS was unlike traditional field days where students are organized into teams and compete against each other in events. She says at IDS students worked together to have fun and achieve success as partners, as they do every day in the classroom.

"One of the things that made Field Day really great," says Coach Kathy, "is that it was another one of those special times when the older students rose to the occasion and really gave of themselves to the younger students. In addition, we had a supportive group of parents that made it all possible and served as a tremendous model of cooperation and teamwork for our students."

IDS Hosts Family-Friendly Chamber Music Series

Lake Lipsey shimmers in the afternoon sunlight. Tall oak trees provide shade around the lake's shore. Wild birds swoop and dive into the still water.

Without a doubt, the location of the IDS theater and training center on the school's Lake Lipsey campus is idyllic. The school has added one more element to this exquisite natural setting – the sound of beautiful, classical music.

"Our facility is an ideal place to enjoy performances of classical chamber music," said music teacher Tom McColley. "That's why we were so excited and proud to launch the second season of our own IDS chamber music series designed for the entire family. We called it *Reflections*."

According to Mr. McColley, "The concerts have been an opportunity for families to slow down their frenetic pace and spend time together sharing an experience designed to uplift, educate and enlighten – listening to the live performance of beautiful music."

Professional musicians who perform in some of Florida's finest orchestras were invited to participate in the series of three concerts. One concert, *Reflections Brass*, featured top symphonic brass musicians playing a variety of music from several centuries.

The second concert featured the Florida Orchestra's associate concert master, violinist Stewart Kitts. Kitts and other top musicians performed Igor Stravinsky's "L'histoire du Soldat" ("A Soldier's Tale"). The third concert, *Mostly Mozart*, included Mozart's Flute Quartet, as well as one of the most famous string quartets ever written, "Eine Kleine Nachtmusik."

Prior to each concert, IDS teachers provided students with an overview of the featured presentation. "We work with the series as an extension of the classroom, so that the concerts become more meaningful for them," said Mr. McColley.

While many IDS families attended the performances, many members of the community found them to be enjoyable, as well. IDS is unique in the North Tampa area in providing quality, classical musical performances, according to Mr. McColley. "IDS is proud to share its facility. We look forward to continuing these types of events, and becoming a center for quality music and culture in our community."

IDS Celebrates Music and Art Around the World

On a spectacular Thursday evening in December, students at IDS took their families and friends on a musical and artistic world tour, as they celebrated Fine Arts Night with an international flair. The title of the program was "What a Wonderful World," from the song made popular by Louis Armstrong.

"Students showcased music from an incredible variety of cultures. The Spirit Catchers, beginning and advanced bands and the sixth grade World Drum Ensemble, performed folk songs and dances from South Africa, France, Israel, India, Japan, Ireland, England, South America and the United States," according to music teacher Tom McColley. McColley and music and computer teacher Michael LeBlanc organized the program.

Students from every grade level, ranging from Pre-Kindergarten to seventh grade, contributed cultural crafts from the same countries that were featured musically. In their art classes, they created projects ranging from Japanese kites and origami to Native American masks and African rain sticks. The Art Club also contributed, with a display of French quilling and headbands worn by the drummers.

Debbie Kerr and Susan Bossard, art teachers at the school, assigned each grade level a country. Students researched that country to learn how its people expressed themselves through art.

"One of the goals at IDS is to help students to understand their own cultural heritage and the heritage of other world cultures," said Bossard. "One of the ways we do that is through an appreciation of the arts," she said.

"At IDS, another guiding principle is to teach the whole child," said Kerr. "This means providing seamless learning experiences in which courses are not considered as separated, isolated subjects, but as an integrated curriculum in which music, art and social studies are inter-related."

"When you travel to another country," said Bossard, "you learn its geography, study its history and appreciate its culture through the fine arts – its songs and dances, native costumes, painting, sculpture and other decorative arts and crafts. Our students are learning about other countries the same way."

Sergio Waksman, the father of a participating second grade student, said, "It is quite an accomplishment when young children are able to enjoy and value diversity." With a strong sense of their own heritage and a healthy appreciation for other cultures, students at IDS know "What a Wonderful World" this can be.

Student-Led Conferences Celebrate Success, Teach Life-Long Skills

When it's time for conferences at IDS, students take charge. Adding a new dimension to the traditional parent/teacher-only approach to conferences, IDS students – some as young as first grade – have the opportunity to play an integral role in evaluating their progress, setting goals, and discussing it with their parents.

The method used to engage children in this process is student-led conferences, and according to teachers, parents and students alike, the benefits are tremendous. "Student-led conferences at IDS are really a celebration of all the wonderful things our children do," said primary multiage teacher Jennifer Jones. "It's parents and teachers coming together to empower students and help them become the best they can be."

"We are always working to develop the student/teacher/parent team," said Middle School Division Leader Betty George. "Student-led conferences are a wonderful way of strengthening the student part of that team."

Student-led conferences instill pride by encouraging responsibility and ownership. They foster self-awareness and help build confidence and trust. With teachers at their side for support and encouragement, students explain what they're learning to their parents, while demonstrating important analytical, critical thinking, and communication skills they'll be using throughout their lives.

"As our students move on to high school, they will be taking more and more responsibility for their own education," said George. "Helping them to self-assess and to plan and work toward a goal is an important life-long skill."

Beginning with some primary classes, and including the entire intermediate and middle school divisions, teachers carefully prepare students for their conferences. Students create portfolios of current work, and teachers coach them on how to discuss the work with their parents while following a preset agenda. According to fourth grade teacher Vickii Ausburn, this preparation enables the conference to become "a powerful experience for the students to showcase their academic work and abilities."

Fourth grade parent Paul Stach, said his daughter "took her conference seriously. She was thorough and enthusiastic in her explanations." Barbara MacBride, parent of a fourth-grader, said her son "demonstrated a real love for learning as he proudly showed me his portfolio."

As part of their preparation, students conduct a self-evaluation of their academic progress and classroom behavior – a critical element of the conference learning experience. "How students perceive themselves has a big impact on their academic performance," said first grade teacher Kim Fowler. Younger students think about issues such as how often they share and take turns, or if they're friendly and polite. Older students focus on specific skills and subject areas, as well as work habits.

"It has become clear that taking time for reflection before moving on to new topics is a brain friendly thing to do," said fifth grade teacher and Intermediate Division

Leader Michelle Hill. "Evaluating their work sharpens students' analytical skills, and improves their ability to monitor their own progress."

"Student-led conferences provide a dynamic opportunity for students to assess their strengths as well as their areas of challenge," said Hill's teaching partner and Director of Studies, Linda Wenzel. They believe the experience provides a solid bridge to middle school for fifth graders by focusing them on actions and consequences, and increasing their awareness of what they need to do to get the results they want. Their students agree.

"I like student-led conferences because our parents get to hear our opinions about our work and how we plan to improve," said one fifth-grader.

"I believe that student-led conferences are much better," said another student. "I love being in charge and I enjoy telling my parents about my school work in my own personal way."

PFA Runs on Commitment, Community and Camaraderie

Walk across the IDS campus on any given day and try to count the number of parent volunteers. They're in the kitchen preparing lunch, in the library checking out books, in the classrooms stuffing Thursday folders, helping with centers, or providing teachers with an extra set of hands. They're by the grills flipping burgers for a class cookout, and they're in the copy room, well, copying.

And if you look in a small room in the back of Corbett Hall, you might find the "brain trust" of all this activity –

the Executive Committee of the IDS Parent Faculty Association (PFA). That's only if these officers are having a meeting – otherwise, they're out on campus, themselves, in the kitchen, the library, the classrooms, by the grills, in the copy room, or just about anywhere else they can help out.

While the scope of activity in which parents are involved at IDS is wide and varied, ask any of these members of the Executive Committee what the fundamental role of the PFA is, and the answer is unanimous – to help raise funds for special school needs that directly affect students. It's a role the PFA has filled year after year with incredible success, having a lasting impact on both students and the quality of education at IDS.

The lunch program. The Big Event. The Kids Golf Classic. Booster Club and gift wrap sales. From each class basket that is created for the annual auction, to every coke float, snow cone, hot dog or taco that is served, the combined efforts of all parents, grandparents and friends of IDS volunteering through numerous programs make a dramatic difference at IDS.

While fund-raising is, indeed, the PFA's most time consuming activity, there's an important outgrowth of that intensive effort that's impossible to list in an annual report or an accounting spreadsheet. Most would agree it's even more important to children than new swings and slides.

That is the sense of community, sharing, and teamwork volunteers create to provide an example of the IDS philosophy for students. Personal responsibility. Making positive contributions. Hands-on participation.

"The primary goal of the PFA is to facilitate communication between parents and teachers," says current PFA President Dawn Schocken. "A second goal is to provide fund-raising activities. And a third is to help create a sense of community among parents, faculty and staff."

"We serve as a model for our children," says Janet Stewart, immediate past president of the PFA. "When they see us volunteering, that serves as an example that they can carry throughout their lives."

After all, as PFA Vice President Bob Rocco says, "It's all about the children."

COMMUNITY SERVICE
&
TRAINING FOR EXCELLENCE

Providing Community Service With a Smile!

In true IDS tradition, students, teachers and staff reached out to the community throughout the year in a wide variety of ways – through volunteering their time and talent to important causes, offering quality cultural programs, and extending a thoughtful, caring hand to those less fortunate.

Models of this special IDS kind of caring for the community abound in every grade and in every class. One example is the annual middle school Community Service Day. Each year, students decide where they will spend their time on this day and what specific contributions they would like to make. This year, middle schoolers worked throughout the area on this special day of caring by spending time with the disabled, cleaning up the environment, helping the elderly, and sorting clothes for the needy.

When primary division students celebrated Centifest – the 100ᵗʰ day of school – they participated in a wide variety of activities involving the number 100. One of the most rewarding was the creation of 100 valentines, which were distributed to patients at University Community Hospital – a gesture that was greatly appreciated by hospital patients and staff.

"Your students helped brighten the day for many of our patients," wrote one hospital representative.

On Pond Day, seventh graders pitched in and literally "got their feet wet" helping the environment by restoring the IDS pond to its native wetland state. This tradition continues to be a highlight of the seventh grade curriculum.

A special project for third graders gave them the opportunity to apply skills in marketing, finance, teamwork, and problem-solving – while helping children less fortunate. Creating, producing, selling and delivering candygrams prior to the winter holidays resulted in $800 – all of which students enthusiastically donated to a children's home in Tampa.

The children's home was also the beneficiary of the Intermediate Student Council's community service efforts this year. The council coordinated drives during the year to collect items, including paper goods and cleaning supplies that are needed by the home and always in short supply.

A local shelter for abused women and their children, is another organization that has been "adopted" by the IDS community. In addition to the annual drive during the winter holidays to collect gifts and necessities for families who are starting out on their own, the second grade "Top Bananas" earmarked the profits from their annual chocolate factory sales for this organization.

Another highlight of community sharing at IDS this year was the *Reflections* classical music concert series. The school opened its doors to offer a delightful cultural event for families on Sunday afternoons, three times during the school year.

These are just a few of the many hands-on, community service related projects that take place throughout the year in each classroom at IDS. They're lessons that last a lifetime – lessons in kindness, compassion, and responsibility for others and for one's community.

Nationally Renowned Kagan Structures Modeled at IDS

More than 200 educators from public and private schools across the state of Florida gathered at IDS on January 24-25, 2003, to attend training on the latest strategies for awakening new levels of learning in students and increasing success.

The training, hosted by the University of South Florida's David C. Anchin Center and the Florida Council of Independent Schools, featured internationally-renowned researcher, trainer and author Dr. Spencer Kagan and presenter and author Laurie Kagan. They discussed "Higher Level Thinking and Increased Achievement" and "Cooperative Learning Structures for Success."

Dr. Kagan and his wife, Laurie Kagan, have captured the attention of educators worldwide with innovative research-based learning strategies. These structures give teachers tools to address the individual ways students absorb information and help them reach all types of learners.

"IDS, in recent years, has become a model school for Kagan Cooperative Learning Structures," Dr. Kagan said. "Teachers from around the United States and even other countries have visited IDS to see Kagan structures in action. The power of the structures is not best conveyed by words or pictures, but by seeing the reactions of the students."

Participants explore the caring environment and creative curriculum at IDS as an example of a Kagan model school... The teachers see in action a revolutionary approach to instruction. It's an approach that allows teachers to increase achievement, improve ethnic relations, improve social relations and have students develop character.

The strategies taught in the workshop are research-based. According to Dr. Kagan, over 1,000 studies have proven their effectiveness. The strategies are easy to learn and use. Teachers leave the training with practical techniques they can use the next day. Learning how to incorporate strategies such as multiple intelligences, cooperative learning activities, and higher-level thinking structures into everyday lessons will help teachers evoke peak performance from themselves and their students.

"The Kagan structures pull from the students' higher-level thinking, while they are learning traditional academic content," he said. "The advantage is that no time is taken from academic content and students perform better while teachers utilize the structures."

"As students become better at thinking and caring and learning, they go out into the world better prepared to make good decisions and to create a better world. They are our future," Dr. Kagan said.

Dr. Swarzman said she looks forward to future Kagan workshops at IDS, and the opportunity to welcome teachers to our school to learn, grow and participate in the exciting educational journey. "Each time Dr. Kagan comes, he brings to us the next level of training," she said. "This enhances our emphasis on creating a brain-friendly environment to even better inspire learning."

"We consider teacher training to be at the heart of education," she emphasized. "We're excited to offer this workshop for the sixth consecutive year to showcase the best and most exciting teaching techniques – and give visiting educators the opportunity to explore the caring environment and creative curriculum our teachers work so hard to provide."

Middle School Retreat Provides Opportunities for Learning and Community Building

By the time it was over, students had dubbed the two-day retreat "Boot Camp for Middle Schoolers." While the hours of training were long and intense, the lessons learned were timeless – cooperation, respect, and dignity for others.

The IDS Middle School retreat, held on the school campus in August, was modeled after adult business training programs, "but for young adults," added Dr. Joyce Swarzman, IDS headmaster, who led the session with Betty George, Middle School Division Leader, and the entire Middle School faculty. The goal, Swarzman said, was "to create high expectations for learning and interacting with each other in a way that promotes dignity and respect for all."

Using Stephen Covey's book, *The Seven Habits of Highly Effective Teens*, as a guide throughout the retreat, participants discussed individual learning styles (Kinesthetic, Tactual, Auditory and Visual) and the need to develop an appreciation for the learning styles of others. "Communication for Effective Interaction" and "Study Skills for Success" were covered, as participants worked towards building a strong learning community that honors the rights of all learners to excel both academically and emotionally.

Even a few months later, the glow of camaraderie and caring developed during the two days of learning and community building continues when Middle School students discuss the retreat with enthusiasm and laughter.

"The emphasis on learning styles has helped me study better and become a better student," said one student.

According to another student, the insight she gained during a "Choose Your Attitude" discussion has helped her develop win-win situations, even when she's having a bad day.

For a third student, the greatest benefit of the retreat has been "that now we respect each other more. We're even more like a family."

A Summary of the 7 Components of the *M.O.R.E. Approach*

Component I: Child-Centered Vision

The information in this component supports a direction that facilitates a more joyful and effortless learning community, by leaning heavily on the change process and lessons from neurobiologists to accelerate learning.

Component II: Appreciating the Uniqueness of the Learner

Understanding the different learning styles, whereby people intake and process information through learning preferences, is the foundation for creating a learning environment in which all students are able and expected to succeed. Academic, behavioral, social and emotional styles are included.

Component III: Motivational Strategies to Increase Time On Task

Research on effective teaching adds credence to the obvious–the more time students spend on task, the higher the comprehension and greater the achievement. In order to increase time on task, IDS teachers make full use of an array of brain-friendly strategies and gimmicks to capture student interest, mix fun into the learning process and bring learning to life.

Component IV: Creating Dignity and Respect

PMS: a positive mental set and positive phrasing are at the heart of all interactions at IDS. Faculty and staff work to focus on what they want people to know or do. Having a positive approach involves choosing options and seeking solutions, rather than creating and dwelling on obstacles. Seeing the glass as half full, rather than half empty takes more than words and knowledge; it takes commitment and team support to "walk the talk" in order to bring this philosophy to life. Core values are emphasized along with specific communication skills to support an environment that adds credence to the power of dignity and respect.

Component V: Teacher Presence, Making Connections

Research supports the long-held belief that the teacher makes the difference in setting the tone, culture and academic success in the classroom. Teacher presence represents the nonverbal behaviors and mental set that send a message to the student about the teacher's intention, subconscious confidence and ability to make strong connections with the learner. Teacher presence that conveys both "I care" and "I am the teacher" provides the leadership that every child deserves.

Component VI: Learning Community

IDS uses cooperative learning models, team instruction and communication strategies that enhance group dynamics to create a synergistic, cohesive and successful learning community. A vibrant learning community includes teachers, parents and students in the process. IDS also seeks to distinguish itself as a private institution with a public purpose – sharing our success with the greater educational community.

Component VII: Curriculum Development

IDS teachers incorporate into their thought processes a wide array of components that deserve attention when organizing and implementing effective curriculum plans. At the heart of curriculum development is the intention to engage students meaningfully, while creating a comprehensive framework for classroom application. The use of multiple learning strategies woven into a seamless plan can lead to elegant teaching and insightful learning opportunities.

Resources

Anderson, Ole, Marsh, M. & Harvey, Dr. A. Learn with the Classics: Using Music To Study Smart at Any Age. San Francisco: Lind Institute, 1999. *(**includes a uniquely designed music CD**)*

Anderson, Robert H. & Pavan, Barbara Nelson. Nongradedness. Lancaster, PA: Technomic Publishing Company, Inc., 1993.

Armstrong, Thomas. Multiple Intelligences in the Classroom. Alexandria, VA: Association for Supervision and Curriculum Development,1994.

Bethel, Sheila Murray. Making a Difference: Twelve Qualities That Make You a Leader. New York: Berkley Books, 1990.

Blanchard, Ken. High Five! New York, N.Y.: HarperCollins Publishers Inc., 2001.

Boothman, Nicholas. How to make people like you in 90 seconds or less. New York: Workman Publishing, 2000.

Borba, Ed.D., Michele. Building Moral Intelligence. San Francisco, CA.: Jossey-Bass, 2001.

Caine, Renate Nummela & Caine, Geoffrey. Making Connections: Teaching and the Human Brain. Alexandria, VA: Association for Supervision and Curriculum Development, 1991.

Campbell, Don. The Mozart Effect. New York, N.Y.: Avon Books Inc., 1997.

Clem, Stephen C. and Wilson, Z. Vance. Paths to New Curriculum. Washington, D.C.: National Association of Independent Schools (NAIS), 1991.

Cohen, Debbie Happy. Reach Your Stars! A guide to fulfill your dreams, not someday, but NOW! Miami, FL: Bee Happy Publishing, 2002.

Coles, Robert. The Moral Intelligence of Children. New York: The Penguin Group, 1998.

Covey, Stephen R. The Seven Habits of Highly Effective People. New York: Simon & Schuster, 1990.

Covey, Stephen R. Principle-Centered Leadership. New York, N.Y.: Simon & Schuster, 1990.

Curwin, Richard L. & Mendler, Allen N. Discipline with Dignity. Alexandria, VA: Association for Supervision and Curriculum Development,1998.

Danielson, Charlotte. Enhancing Professional Practice: A Framework for Teaching. Alexandria, VA: Association for Supervision and Curriculum Development,1996.

Dennison, Ph.D., Paul E. and Dennison, Gail E. Brain Gym. Ventura, CA. Edu-Kinesthetics Inc., 1994.

DePorter, Bobbi, Reardon, Mark & Singer-Nourie, Sarah. Quantum Teaching. Needham Heights, MA: Allyn & Bacon, 1999.

Drucker, Peter F. Managing For the Future: 1990's and Beyond. New York: The Penguin Group, 1992.

Dryden, Gordon and Vos, Dr. Jeannette. The Learning Revolution. Torrance, CA.: The Learning Web, 1999.

Gardner, Howard. Multiple Intelligences: The Theory in Practice. New York: HarperCollins Publishers, Inc.,1993.

Glasser, M.D., William. Control Theory in the Classroom. New York: Harper & Row, 1986.

Glasser, M.D., William. Schools Without Failure. New York: Harper & Row, 1975.

Goleman, Daniel. Emotional Intelligence. New York: Bantam Books, 1997.

Goodlad, John I. & Anderson Robert H. The Non-Graded Elementary School, Revised Edition. New York: Teachers College Press, 1987.

Haberman, Martin. Star Teachers of Children in Poverty. West Lafayette, IN: Kappa Delta Pi, 1995.

Hannaford, Ph.D., Carla. Smart Moves: Why Learning Is Not All In Your Head. Arlington, VA: Great Ocean Publishers, 1995.

Harmin, Merrill. Inspiring Active Learning: A Handbook for Teachers. Alexandria, VA: Association for Supervision and Curriculum Development, 1994.

Hart, Leslie A. Human Brain and Human Learning. Village of Oak Creek, AZ: Books for Educators, 1991.

Hyerle, David. Visual Tools for Constructing Knowledge. Alexandria, VA: Association for Supervision and Curriculum Development, 1996.

Jacobs, Heidi Hayes, ed. Interdisciplinary Curriculum: Design and Implementation. Alexandria, VA: Association for Supervision and Curriculum Development,1989.

Jensen, Eric. Arts with the Brain in Mind. Alexandria, VA.: Association for Supervision and Curriculum Development (ASCD), 2001.

Jensen, Eric. Super Teaching. Del Mar, CA: Turning Point Publishing, 1995.
Jensen, Eric. Teaching with the Brain in Mind. Alexandria, VA: Association for Supervision and Curriculum Development,1998.
Johnson, M.D., Spencer. Who Moved My Cheese? New York: G.P. Putnam's Sons, 1998.
Kagan, Ph.D., Dr. Spencer. Cooperative Learning. San Juan Capistrano, CA.: Resources for Teachers, Inc., 1992, 1994.
Kagan, Dr. Spencer & Kagan, Miguel. Multiple Intelligences: The Complete MI Book. San Clemente, CA: Kagan Cooperative Learning, 1998.
Kovalik, Susan. ITI: The Model – Integrated Thematic Instruction. 3rd Edition. Kent, WA: Books for Educators, Inc., 1994.
Lieberman, Ann & Miller, Lynne. Teachers, Their World and Their Work: Implications for School Improvement. Alexandria, VA: Association for Supervision and Curriculum Development, 1984.
Marzano, Robert J. A Different Kind of Classroom: Teaching With Dimensions of Learning. Alexandria, VA.: Association for Supervision and Curriculum Development (ASCD), 1992.
Marzano, Robert J., Pickering, Debra J. and Pollock, Jane E. Classroom Instruction That Works. Alexandria, VA.: Association for Supervision and Curriculum Development (ASCD), 2001.
Ostander, Sheila & Schroeder, Lynn. Superlearning. New York: Dell Publishing, 1979.
Performance Learning Systems, Inc. Project T.E.A.C.H. Cadiz, KY.: Association for Supervision and Curriculum Development (ASCD), 1992.
Pert, Candace B. Molecules of Emotion. New York: Simon & Schuster, 1997.
Robbins, Anthony. Unlimited Power. New York: Fawcett Columbine, 1987.
Rose, Colin & Nicholl, Malcolm J. Accelerated Learning for the 21st Century. New York: Dell Publishing, 1997.
Schwartz, Ph.D. David J. The Magic of Thinking Big. New York, Simon & Schuster: 1959.
Sims, M.Ed., Pamela. Awakening Brilliance. Atlanta, GA: Bayhampton Publications, 1997.
Sousa, Dr. David A. How the Brain Learns. Reston, VA: National Association of Secondary School Principals, 1995.

Sprenger, Marilee. Learning & Memory: The Brain In Action. Alexandria, VA.: Association for Supervision and Curriculum Development (ASCD), 1999.

Sylwester, Robert. A Celebration of Neurons: An Educators Guide to the Human Brain. Alexandria, VA: Association for Supervision and Curriculum Development, 1995.

Walton, Mary. The Deming Management Method. New York: Putnam Publishing Group, 1986.

Media Resources

Motivational Videos for In-Staff Development

Bancroft, Ann. "The Vision of Teams." St. Paul, MN: Star Thrower Distribution, 1998. (800) 242-3220

Barker, Joel Arthur. "The Power of Vision." Burnsville, MN: Charthouse International Learning Corp., 1993.

Haebig, Jeff, Ph.D. "Body-Brain Boogie Through Movement." Rochester, MN.: Wellness Quest, 2001.

Kanter, Rosabeth Moss. "Change Masters: Innovations For Productivity in the American Corporation." New York, NY: Simon & Schuster, 1987.

Lundin, Ph.D., Stephen C., and Christensen, John. "FISH." Burnsville, MN: Charthouse Learning Corp., 1998.

Music CDs

"Relax with the Classics: Collection 2, Special Edition." San Francisco, CA: Lind Institute, 1996. (800) 462-3766

IDS Philosophy

"IDS was founded on and remains devoted to the ideal that a happy child... one who is given respect as a unique human being and allowed to fulfill his/her needs to play, to investigate and to be him/herself... is more open to learning than a child who is unhappy, tense and fearful. We consider it our responsibility to foster each child's capacity for learning, to help him/her grow morally, spiritually, and emotionally, as well as physically and intellectually. Recognizing the many differences in learning rates and styles, we believe in individualizing each child's school experience to whatever extent is possible for the fullest development of his/her potential. It is our belief that school should be interesting and even exciting; that each child's work and behavior should be evaluated in terms of his/her own inherent capacity, rather than through comparison with others; and that cooperation is more valuable than competition. Our goal is to provide a relaxed but stimulating atmosphere wherein each child feels acceptance and encouragement in the achievement of success through the exercise of responsible choice."

Founders: Marilyn Gatlin and Betty Anderson
--- 1968

Catch the Spirit at IDS!

IDS remains unique, as it is possible to walk into any classroom at any time of day, every day, with teachers and students warmly greeting visitors. They share what and how they are learning with an energy rich in joy and enthusiasm.

IDS remains unique with an entire faculty and staff who support what they do by possessing a strong respect for best practices and research in education.

IDS remains unique because we seek to implement best practices **ALL** at once. We Study, Implement, Refine, Implement, and repeat the cycle over and over again as a continuous refinement process.

This model has led to much success with students, has been an inspiration to other educators and has provided a challenge to us to always seek unlimited options that align with a happy, growing, human gift – a "child."

Quotes like, "Turn every problem into an opportunity," or "Every problem has a solution" are **NOT** clichés at IDS; **they are a way of life!**

We believe that every school can share in this way of life. A positively phrased adaptation of Margaret Mead's famous quote points us in the right direction:

"Always believe that a small group of thoughtful, committed people can change the world. Indeed, it's the only thing that ever has."

Services Available

Founded in 1968, IDS, recently renamed *Independent Day School: Corbett Campus*, is a fully accredited, non-sectarian, independent school located in northwest Hillsborough County. It serves 500 plus students in grades Pre-K through 8. At IDS, all children experience learning in a highly academic and nurturing environment focused on excellence and developing a positive self-concept. IDS has become recognized as an exemplary school, capturing the interest of teachers and educational leaders who have come to observe and learn from and with IDS teachers.

A private school with a public purpose (we are a nonprofit organization, a 501(c)(3)), our primary focus is serving our children. Our second purpose is to have a positive impact on the greater community to benefit students everywhere. What started in 1968 as a commitment in education to treat each child as a unique individual has transformed into a state of the art educational hub, where teachers are trained in the latest brain-based research, so that they can bring out the best in *each and every student*.

IDS has an idyllic training facility and offers leading-edge workshops year-round. For more information about our *M.O.R.E. Approach* educational workshops and materials, or to inquire about sending your children to IDS, please call: **(813) 961-3087**. You can also visit us at **www.idsyes.com**.